W9-ARI-252

Euripides: Bacchae

Euripides
Bacchae

A new translation and
commentary by David Franklin

Introduction to the Greek Theatre
by P.E. Easterling

Series Editors: John Harrison and Judith Affleck

CAMBRIDGE
UNIVERSITY PRESS

PUBLISHED BY THE PRESS SYNDICATE OF THE UNIVERSITY OF CAMBRIDGE
The Pitt Building, Trumpington Street, Cambridge, United Kingdom

CAMBRIDGE UNIVERSITY PRESS
The Edinburgh Building, Cambridge CB2 2RU, UK   http://www.cup.cam.ac.uk
40 West 20th Street, New York, NY 10011–4211, USA   http://www.cup.org
10 Stamford Road, Oakleigh, Melbourne 3166, Australia
Ruiz de Alarcón 13, 28014 Madrid, Spain

© Cambridge University Press 2000

This book is in copyright. Subject to statutory exception and to the provisions
of relevant collective licensing agreements, no reproduction of any part may
take place without the written permission of Cambridge University Press.

First published 2000

Printed in the United Kingdom at The University Press, Cambridge

Typeface Minion   *System* QuarkXPress®

A catalogue record for this book is available from the British Library

ISBN 0 521 65372 X paperback

ACKNOWLEDGEMENTS
Thanks are due to the following for permission to reproduce pictures:

p. 6 courtesy of the Arthur M. Sackler Museum, Harvard University Art
Museums. Bequest of David M. Robinson. Photographer Michael Nedzweski.
© President and Fellows of Harvard College; pp. 24, 50, 82 Richard Feldman;
p. 42 courtesy of the University Museums, University of Mississippi Cultural
Center. Photographer Maria Daniels; p. 92 Musée de la civilisation
gallo-romaine, Lyon (France). Photographer Christian Thioc.

p. 98, Fig. A from *The Cambridge Ancient History, Plates to Volumes V and VI.*

Map on p. viii by Helen Humphreys.

Cover photograph: Caravaggio's Baccho, Archiv Alinari, Firenze.

Performance
For permission to give a public performance of *Bacchae* please
write to Permissions Department, Cambridge University Press,
The Edinburgh Building, Shaftesbury Road, Cambridge CB2 2RU.

Contents

Preface

The aim of the series is to enable students to approach Classical plays with confidence and understanding; to discover the play within the text.

The translations are new. Many recent versions of Greek tragedy have been done by poets and playwrights who do not work from the original Greek. The translators of this series aim to bring readers, actors and directors as close as possible to the playwrights' actual words and intentions: to create translations which are faithful to the original in content and tone; and which are speakable, with all the immediacy of modern English.

The notes are designed for students of Classical Civilisation and Drama, and indeed anyone who is interested in theatre. They address points which present difficulty to the reader of today; chiefly relating to the Greeks' religious and moral attitudes, their social and political life, and mythology.

Our hope is that students should discover the play for themselves. The conventions of the Classical theatre are discussed, but there is no thought of recommending 'authentic' performances. Different groups will find different ways of responding to each play. The best way of bringing alive an ancient play, as any other, is to explore the text practically, to stimulate thought about ways of staging the plays today. Stage directions in the text are minimal, and the notes are not prescriptive; rather, they contain questions and exercises which explore the dramatic qualities of the text. Bullet points introduce suggestions for discussion and analysis; open bullet points focus on more practical exercises.

If the series encourages students to attempt a staged production, so much the better. But the primary aim is understanding and enjoyment.

This translation of *Bacchae* is based on the Oxford University Press text, edited by G. Murray.

John Harrison
Judith Affleck

Background to the story of Bacchae

Bacchae was one of Euripides' last plays, written in Macedonia at the court of King Archelaus. After Euripides' death in 406 BC, the play was brought to Athens and performed at the City Dionysia (the god's annual festival, held in the Theatre of Dionysus) in 405 BC. It won first prize.

Nearly all of the important characters of this play, divine and human, are related. The gods' names are in bold type:

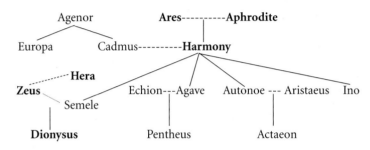

Agenor, king of Tyre in Syria, sent **Cadmus** and his brothers to look for their sister Europa, who had been carried off by Zeus. Cadmus came to Delphi and was told to found a city in the place to which he was led by a cow. The cow lay down on the site of Thebes, where Cadmus killed a dragon and sowed its teeth in the ground. The teeth grew into armed soldiers, but Cadmus made them fight each other until only five were left. These *Spartoi* (Sown Men) became the nobility of Thebes.

On his travels, Cadmus had rescued Zeus himself from Typhon, a monster born of the Earth. Zeus rewarded him with a divine bride, Harmony. In time, Cadmus gave their daughter **Agave** in marriage to one of the *Spartoi*, Echion. Echion and Agave became the parents of **Pentheus**.

When Zeus had an affair with Semele, his wife Hera was jealous, and so she made Semele doubt that her lover was really Zeus. Semele made Zeus swear to grant her a wish, and when he did, she asked him to reveal himself as a god. Zeus had to do so, and Semele was destroyed by the lightning blast of his radiance. Zeus took her unborn baby **Dionysus** and sewed him into his own thigh, until he was born again (the name Dionysus was often taken to mean 'twice-born').

Although born in Thebes, Dionysus came to Greece as a foreigner, from Phrygia in Persia. He was worshipped there as a god of nature and fertility, and his other name, Bacchus, is a word from neighbouring Lydia. Tradition suggests that he came to Greece via Thrace, where he killed Lycurgus, the savage king who resisted the new god. Arriving in

Thebes, his birthplace, Dionysus meets the hostility of the young king Pentheus, also a grandson of Cadmus, and so Dionysus' own cousin. It is clear from the start that the confrontation between these two will be the focus of the drama.

Map of Ancient Greece

List of characters

DIONYSUS   *god of wild nature and wine, son of Zeus*

CHORUS   *Persian women, the Bacchants*

TIRESIAS   *a prophet*

CADMUS   *an old man, grandfather of Pentheus and Dionysus and founder of Thebes*

PENTHEUS   *King of Thebes, Dionysus' cousin*

SOLDIER

FIRST MESSENGER

SECOND MESSENGER

AGAVE   *mother of Pentheus, daughter of Cadmus*

Scene from the American Repertory Theater's 1998 production: Dionysus and the bacchants (left); Pentheus and his men (right).

1

PROLOGUE (1–48)

Divine prologues

The prologue was the opening scene before the Chorus entered. Euripides often opened with a single character explaining what is going on (unlike Sophocles, who preferred dialogue). Gods deliver prologues in several Euripidean plays (e.g. *Trojan Women* and *Hippolytus*), but only in *Bacchae* does the god stay on to play a major role. Here Dionysus announces his purpose (30–2) and sets the scene – Pentheus' palace in Thebes.

● In what ways does such a monologue differ from a dialogue in terms of the audience's relation to the play? What advantages does each have?

1 the land of Thebes We know of many tragedies set in Thebes, Athens' neighbour, but none in Athens itself, except the celebratory *Eumenides*. Perhaps the Athenians did not want a mythical history of disaster tainting their city.

Dionysus

Dionysus' appearance is important and reflects his ambiguous nature, defying such categories as divine/human, Greek/foreign, male/female. He is a god in human form; although born in Thebes, he wears exotic Persian clothes; he is male, but his beauty will be called effeminate; he comes to punish, but his mask wears a serene smile. Dionysus was the god of drama, and this play was first performed in the Theatre of Dionysus in Athens; costume, disguise and illusion are a vital part of him, his theatre, and this play.

7 the undying crime Hera's trick killed Semele (see Background to the story, page vii).

19 the thyrsus This is the main symbol of Dionysiac worship: ivy leaves were pressed into the hollow end of a fennel staff, and sometimes also wound around its stem. It was not sharpened; **spear of ivy** might be just a poetic phrase, but it could also be ominous.

Nemesis

Semele's sisters did not choose to worship Dionysus – he has made them mad as a punishment for denying his divinity. He then reveals that he has driven out *all* the women of Thebes. They did not offend him as personally as Semele's sisters did, but they still refused to worship him. The theme of rejecting a god appears repeatedly in Greek myths. Inevitably such blasphemous arrogance, *hubris*, leads to *nemesis* – destruction. Dionysus now singles out the offence of his most powerful opponent, Pentheus.

BACCHAE

DIONYSUS I, Dionysus, son of Zeus, have come to the land of Thebes!
Semele, the daughter of Cadmus, gave birth to me on the day she was sent into
labour by the fire of lightning. I have put aside my divine form, and in the body
of a man I have come here, to the stream of Dirce and the waters of Ismenus.
Here, by the palace, I see the tomb of my mother where she was struck by   5
that lightning, and the ruins of her house, still smoking with the living
flame of the fire of Zeus – the undying crime of Hera against my mother.
Cadmus, however, I praise, for he has declared this place sacred as his
daughter's shrine. I myself have covered it over with the green clusters of a
vine.   10

   I have left the gold-rich flood plains of Lydia and Phrygia, and travelled
through the sun-beaten uplands of Persia, the walled cities of Bactria and the
fearful country of the Medes, to rich Arabia and all of Asia that lies along the
shores of the sea, its fair-towered cities filled with Greeks and barbarians
mingling together. This is the first Greek city I have come to, after teaching   15
my dances and establishing my rites there in Asia, so that I might be
revealed to mankind as a god.

   So in this land of Greece itself, it is Thebes I have first set ringing with
cries, dressed the people in fawnskins, and put the thyrsus, the spear of ivy,
into their hands; for my mother's sisters, the last people who should have   20
done so, declared that Dionysus was not the son of Zeus. They said that
Semele had slept with a mortal man, and then, on Cadmus' clever
suggestion, blamed Zeus for her sexual shame; and for that reason, they
gloated, Zeus killed her, because she had lied about a marriage with him.
This is why I have stung them into a frenzy, making them leave their homes   25
to live on the mountain, out of their minds. I have compelled them to wear
the clothes of my wild rites, and I have driven all the women of Cadmus' city
– but only the women – in madness from their homes. They have now joined
the daughters of Cadmus, sitting on bare rock under the green pine trees.
This city must learn its lesson well, even against its will, for not celebrating   30
my rites; and I must vindicate my mother Semele, by appearing to mankind
as the god she bore to Zeus.

   Cadmus has passed on his throne and power to his daughter's son,
Pentheus, who now fights with gods – with me! – leaving me out of his
sacrifices, and making no mention of me in his prayers. For this reason   35

40 maenad This originally meant 'mad woman', but the term came to be synonymous with bacchants – women inspired by Dionysus.

42 Tmolus This was a great ridge of mountains in Lydia protecting and dominating the city of Sardis (see map, page viii). Lydian bacchants danced on its slopes.

45 mother Rhea Rhea was Zeus' mother, and so Dionysus' grandmother. She is linked to the Asiatic goddess Cybele, as both were worshipped as earth-goddesses (see note on line 65).

Cithaeron
Mount Cithaeron, just outside Thebes, is the location of many myths. The baby Oedipus was abandoned there, and it was also the scene of Actaeon's death (see note on line 190).

PARODOS (ENTRY OF THE CHORUS) (49–142)
The appearance of the Chorus was an exciting moment. They were highly trained singers and dancers, and often wore magnificent costumes. Their annual performances would have been a high point in the year for the Athenians (see Introduction to the Greek Theatre, page 97).

In most tragedies, the Chorus are conventional inhabitants of the location of the play. This Chorus consists of bacchants, Asian women dancing ecstatically for their leader and god. They call everyone present to worship Dionysus with them. That call must have meant something special to the audience in the Theatre of Dionysus.

51 my joyful labours for Bromios Bromios is a cult name of Dionysus. It means 'the Thunderer', drawing attention to his wildness and power.

53 Bacchus This is another name for Dionysus – hence *Bacchae*, or bacchants.

56 the reverence of holy silence Those in charge of religious occasions called for silence. The call might also draw the audience into the play.

61 The Chorus explain what they mean by reverence (i.e. worship of and respect for the gods). The relationship between mortals and gods is crucial in this play.

65 great mother Cybele Cybele was a Persian mother-goddess embodying the fertility of the earth (compare with the Greek goddess Demeter, see note on line 223). Euripides freely associates Dionysus with other eastern fertility cults.

I will prove to him and to all the Thebans that I am a god. When I have put things right here, I will move on to another land, and reveal myself there also. But if in anger the city of Thebes attempts to take the bacchants from the mountain with military force, I shall fight them, commanding my maenads. So it is that I have put aside my true form, and taken on the likeness of a mortal man. 40

But now, my women who have left Tmolus, the great stronghold of Lydia; my holy band of worshippers, you I have brought from a foreign land as my companions in travel and rest! Lift the native Phrygian drums that mother Rhea and I invented! Come to this royal house of Pentheus, and pound on the doors, to reveal yourselves to the city of Cadmus! I myself will go to the ravines of Cithaeron where my bacchants wait, and I will set them dancing! 45

CHORUS	From the land of Asia,

          Leaving sacred Tmolus behind, 50
       I rush on in my joyful labours for Bromios,
           Work that does not weary me,
           Singing in worship of Bacchus.
         You in the road, you in the road,
         And you in the palace, make way! 55
      Let all show the reverence of holy silence.
       For endlessly the time-honoured hymns
           I'll sing to Dionysus.

        Blessed is he who in his good fortune
          Knows the rites of the god; 60
          Who leads a life of reverence;
       Whose spirit is one with the sacred band;
         Who dances in the mountains
           In the holy rituals;
    Who honours the rites of great mother Cybele; 65
       Waving the thyrsus high in the air,
           Garlanded with ivy,
         He worships Dionysus.

69 On, bacchants! Repeated cries form part of Dionysiac ritual, just as repetition does in the prayer of most cultures (see also line 100). The rhythm of the chant would add to its force, and it is not difficult to imagine that dance added visual power to the words.

72–3 From the mountains of Phrygia The bacchants come from the wildness of Persian mountains to the civic, orderly streets of Greece; the clash of cultures might be disastrous.

74–88 The Chorus tell again the story of Dionysus' miraculous birth.

85 with the horns of a bull For the first time in the play, Dionysus is associated with an animal. The bull is his dominant animal incarnation (see also lines 778–80).

86 garlands of snakes Euripides explains why maenads entwine snakes in their hair in honour of Dionysus.

This vase, dating from c.440–430 BC, shows Dionysus holding thyrsus and wine cup, with satyr and maenad playing musical instruments.

97 the staff of wildness While holiness and wildness may seem at opposite extremes to us, their combination powerfully expresses the nature of Dionysiac worship.

102 Far from their shuttles and looms Weaving was the normal, civilised occupation of women; something extraordinary has happened to the women of Thebes.

On, bacchants! On, bacchants!
Escort Dionysus,   70
Bromios, god and son of god,
From the mountains of Phrygia
Down to the broad streets of Greece – Bromios!

When his mother was carrying him,
The lightning of Zeus flashed through the sky,   75
And in the forcing agony of labour
She thrust him prematurely from her womb,
Losing her life at the thunderbolt's blast.
But instantly Zeus, the son of Cronus
Took him to another place of birth;   80
Concealing the baby within his thigh,
He fastened him in with golden clasps,
Hidden away from Hera.

Zeus brought him to birth when the Fates decreed it,
A god with the horns of a bull,   85
And he crowned the child with garlands of snakes.
And so it is that the maenads entwine
These untameable beasts in their hair.

Thebes, nurse of Semele,
Crown yourself with ivy!   90
Everywhere, everywhere sport the green
Of bryony with its beautiful berries,
And let all become bacchants,
With boughs of oak and fir,
And decorate cloaks of dappled fawnskin   95
With fringes of white wool.
Make yourselves holy with the staff of wildness!
At once the whole land will dance –
It is Bromios who leads the holy bands!
To the mountain, to the mountain!   100
There where the throng of women waits,
Far from their shuttles and looms,
Stung to madness by Dionysus.

104 the Curetes These minor divinities of Crete played a role in the story of Zeus' birth. Like his son Dionysus, Zeus was born amid danger and concealment. His father Cronus feared the fulfilment of a prophecy that he would be overthrown by his son, and so he swallowed his children as soon as his wife Rhea had given birth. When Zeus was about to be born, Rhea went to Crete and gave birth in a cave. The Curetes beat drums to prevent Cronus from hearing the baby's cries.

Euripides often connected up elements of myth, and so moves easily from the birth of Zeus to the drums played by Dionysus' Chorus to accompany the flute. The Chorus invoke the invention of their musical instruments by their divine forebears.

106 the triple-helmed corybants Corybants were spirits of nature associated with both Cybele and Dionysus. Here they seem to be identified with the Curetes. It is not clear what 'triple-helmed' means; perhaps the strangeness of the idea is an effect Euripides intended.

112 The frenzied satyrs Satyrs were the traditional companions of Dionysus. They were associated with sexual freedom, wine, music and ecstatic dance, and so they were naturally linked with his worship.

115–42 The Chorus praise an imaginary worshipper of Dionysus, who dances to exhaustion among the circling revellers, wears the fawnskin cloak, and eats raw meat. They are praising complete, unrestrained participation in the god's worship.

Oreibasia – mountain dancing

Worshippers of Dionysus took part in wild events in the mountains outside the towns where they lived. They would gather at night in numbers to drink and dance to the loud, rhythmic music of drums and high-pitched flutes. The wildness of the rites culminated in the eating of raw flesh. The dominant emotion for participants was joy. Outsiders, like Pentheus, tended to feel suspicion, revulsion or fear.

In lines 115–42 the Chorus invoke the events and spirit of these rites in their original and mythical form. With the god himself leading the revellers, the earth responds to his fertile magic, flowing with milk, wine and honey. Such miracles will actually take place among the bacchants on Cithaeron (see note on Bacchic rites, page 40).

121 *euoi!* Pronounced *E-woi*, this is the traditional Bacchic cry, encapsulating the ecstatic joy of worshippers calling to their god; hence Dionysus is also called Euios (pronounced *E-wi-os*).

Secret chamber of the Curetes,
Sacred dwelling of Crete that gave birth to Zeus,   105
Where the triple-helmed corybants in their caves
Invented for us this circle of stretched hide!
In the straining dance of ecstasy,
They combined it with the sweet-sounding breath of Phrygian flutes,
And put it in the hands of mother Rhea,   110
A beat for the cries of the bacchants.
The frenzied satyrs took it from the mother goddess,
And made it part of the biennial dance,
In which Dionysus delights.

Dionysus is glad when someone in the mountains   115
Falls to the ground from the whirling bands,
Wearing the sacred cloak of fawnskin,
Hunting the blood of goat-slaughter,
The joy of eating raw flesh,
Racing to the mountains of Phrygia, of Lydia,   120
And the leader is Bromios, *euoi!*
The ground flows with milk, flows with wine,
It flows with the nectar of bees.
The Bacchic god holds high the blazing flame of the pine torch
And lets it stream from the shaft,   125
Fragrant as the smoke of Syrian incense.
With running and dances he spurs on the stragglers,
Rousing them with his call,
Tossing his long, thick hair in the breeze.
Amid the joyful cries he bellows: 130
'On, bacchants! On, bacchants!
Wearing the splendour of gold-flowing Tmolus,
Sing praise to Dionysus
With the sound of the deep-booming drum,
Joyfully singing "*euoi!*" to the god of that cry,   135
With Phrygian calls and incantations,
When the sweet, holy music of the pipes
Sounds out its holy notes,
Accompanying those who journey

141 Joyfully, then The celebratory mood of this worship is clear.

● Animal imagery recurs throughout this play. What ideas does the simile of the foal inspire?

FIRST EPISODE (143–291)

After the joyful singing and athletic dancing of the Chorus, Tiresias, a blind old man, comes onto the stage, perhaps led by a boy as in other plays. From the palace appears Cadmus. Both men are decrepit with age, but nonetheless they are wearing the bacchants' characteristic clothes – fawnskins – and are carrying thyrsi like the Chorus. They even intend to dance!

Tiresias

The blind prophet Tiresias appears in many tragedies, and he has obvious dramatic value. His blindness is linked to his ability to 'see' beyond mortal knowledge, and he provides a kind of objective truthful voice within the conflicts of the drama. But his portrayal is unusual in this play. Not only is it odd that he wears Bacchic clothing; instead of offering simple wisdom, he produces a string of ingenious arguments (see note on Sophistry and rhetoric, page 14).

Cadmus

Cadmus has an extraordinary past, as exiled prince and saviour of Zeus, husband of a goddess and founder of Thebes (see Background to the story, page vii). Despite his mythic status, Euripides turns him into a strikingly human character. Our reaction to him is key to our emotional response to the play.

153–4 I will not grow weary Part of the Dionysiac experience is the release of wildness and energy. Whether Cadmus and Tiresias merely feel rejuvenated or are actually empowered is open to question. Some characters in the play seem to feel the power of the god; others actually demonstrate miraculous physical strength.

162 Are we the only men It is the women of Thebes who have left the city in frenzy, driven mad by Dionysus. Cadmus and Tiresias are unique in Thebes in *choosing* to worship Dionysus.

To the mountain, to the mountain!'   140
Joyfully, then, like a foal with its grazing mother,
The bacchant kicks up her flying feet and leaps!

TIRESIAS Who guards the gates? Call Cadmus from the palace, Cadmus,
son of Agenor, the man who left the city of Sidon to build these towers of
Thebes. Go, someone, tell him that Tiresias wants him. He knows why I   145
have come, what we two old men agreed: to make ourselves a thyrsus each,
put on fawnskins, and garland our heads with ivy wreaths.

CADMUS My good friend – I heard you from inside the palace, and I
recognised the wise voice of a wise man – I have come ready, wearing these
clothes of the god. Dionysus, who has appeared to mankind as a god, is the   150
son of my daughter, and we must honour him as much as we are able.
Where must we go to dance, to dance his steps and shake our grey heads?
You tell me, Tiresias, as one old man to another; for you are wise. I will not
grow weary, night or day, striking the ground with my thyrsus; it is so sweet
to forget that we are old!   155

TIRESIAS You feel the same as I do; I too feel young, and will take
part in the dance.

CADMUS Should we travel to the mountain in a wagon?

TIRESIAS No, that would show the god less honour.

CADMUS I will guide and protect you, though we are both old.   160

TIRESIAS The god will lead us there, and it will not be hard.

CADMUS Are we the only men from the city who will dance for
Bacchus?

TIRESIAS Yes, for we alone have sense; the others are wrong.

CADMUS We are hesitating too long; take my hand.   165

Worship and doubt

168–71 intellectual debates on the gods Contemporary philosophers were questioning the nature and existence of the gods. Euripides was certainly aware of and interested in these arguments, but Tiresias dismisses them. He declares that such rationalism is arrogant and blasphemous, and that the right course of action is to follow tradition. Although worship of Dionysus is new, with no prior tradition in Greece, Tiresias says that they should revere the divine in whatever form it appears, rather than using reason to debate it.

171–2 Will people say
● Is Tiresias embarrassed about what he is doing?

176 Tiresias, since you cannot see Euripides uses Tiresias' blindness to let Cadmus announce the arrival of Pentheus. Such 'stage directions' can seem somewhat contrived.

177 Echion was one of the *Spartoi*, the Sown Men. His name means 'snake' or 'dragon', referring to his origin in the teeth of the dragon (see Background to the story, page vii). Pentheus has succeeded Cadmus as king, but Echion's fate is not mentioned in this play, nor anywhere else.

Tiresias and Cadmus

This is a much-discussed scene, because the tone is so difficult to gauge. Two old men wearing such clothes and attempting to dance could easily be laughable; certainly Pentheus will call them ridiculous.

● Do you think Euripides wrote this as a comic scene to entertain, caricaturing Dionysiac worship?
● Some critics insist that humour damages the power of Greek tragedy, and see the old men's behaviour as admirable. Do you agree?
○ Is the scene more dramatically effective when played for laughs?

Pentheus

The young king appears, enraged by the news that the women of his city have rushed off to the mountains to worship a new god, led by a foreign stranger.

● He gives a vivid description of what he believes the bacchants are up to on Cithaeron; but on what evidence does he base this picture? What do we learn about his character from this speech?

188 Those still at large I will hunt Dionysus has warned that the maenads must not be hunted from the mountain (38–40).

190 Actaeon Artemis, the goddess of hunting, turned Actaeon into a stag, and he was torn apart by his own hounds on Mount Cithaeron (see note on 269–71). He is mentioned several times in this play, where hunters and hunted change places, and his fate will have a still more horrible echo.

TIRESIAS Here, clasp my hand in yours.

CADMUS I do not scorn the gods, since I am mortal myself.

TIRESIAS We do not hold intellectual debates on the gods. No logic
will overthrow the traditions we have received from our fathers,
traditions as old as time, no matter what clever arguments are thought   170
up by the greatest minds. Will people say that I have no sense of what
is proper in old age, going to dance with my head crowned with ivy?
Well, the god has made no distinction as to whether young or old
should dance; he wants to receive equal honour from all, counting
no one out in his desire for worship.   175

CADMUS Tiresias, since you cannot see, I will be your interpreter of
events: Echion's son, Pentheus, the man to whom I have given the
throne of this land, is coming this way, hurrying towards the palace.
How agitated he is! What news will he bring?

PENTHEUS I have been away from this land, but I hear of new evils in   180
the city; that our women have abandoned their homes to take part in fake
Bacchic revels, leaping around in the shadows of the mountains, dancing
to honour this new god, Dionysus – whoever he is. Among the dancing
bands stand full bowls of wine, and one by one the women creep off to
hide in secret places and serve the lusts of men. They claim to be   185
maenads offering sacrifice, but they put Aphrodite before the Bacchic
god. Those I have caught are guarded by warders in the public prison,
their hands bound. Those still at large I will hunt from the mountains –
Ino, and Agave, who bore me to my father Echion; and the mother of
Actaeon – Autonoë, I mean; I will catch them in iron nets and put a   190
stop to this obscene revelry.
   They say that a foreigner has come here, a magical enchanter from the
land of Lydia, his blond hair smelling of perfume, his cheeks flushed, with

194 the charms of Aphrodite Pentheus describes Dionysus in this passage.

● What do Pentheus' words reveal about his preoccupations?

196–7 by cutting his head from his body Like many tragic kings, Pentheus is extreme with his threats (see also 201, 209–10, 281–2).

202 But here The convention of an actor 'noticing' others onstage after delivering a monologue was more common in comedy – which may be relevant here, considering the appearance of Cadmus and Tiresias.

207 *You* have persuaded him Pentheus now turns his hostility against Tiresias. Kings in tragedy often allege corruption against Tiresias when he tells them something they do not want to hear (see Oedipus in *Oedipus Tyrannus*, and Creon in *Antigone*). They are always wrong to do so.

Wine and women

In Aristophanes' comedy *Thesmophoriazusae*, the women of Athens are furious with 'Euripides' for exposing the embarrassing female vice of secret drinking and consequent corruption. Some ancient writers have seen reason to criticise Euripides for misogyny; but bear in mind that the words of his characters do not necessarily represent his own opinions. (See note on Misogyny, page 46.)

Alcohol and other drugs are often seen as a plague of the modern world; but all societies have used mind-altering substances, and sometimes they are regarded as a divine gift.

● What do wine and the theatre, both sacred to Dionysus, have in common?

213 Blasphemy! The Chorus in tragedy usually try to minimise conflict between characters; here they take sides with a vengeance. They are unafraid of the king, and address him as 'stranger' in his own country. That such aggression is voiced by women is also remarkable.

● What difference does their partiality make to the play?

Sophistry and rhetoric (216–20)

The Sophists (Greek *sophos*, intelligent) were intellectuals who made money by giving lectures on a range of subjects. They gained a reputation (at least in comic parody) as slick-tongued but immoral, since they taught how to argue both sides of an argument. Sophistry has come to mean clever but misguided rhetoric. Although Tiresias criticises such ways of speaking (168–71), he himself seems guilty of sophistry (216–61). Of course, the criticism can be and is used to discredit noticeably good speakers.

223 the goddess Demeter Demeter represented the fertility and bounty of the earth (see also notes on lines 45 and 65).

the charms of Aphrodite in his eyes. Day and night he mingles with young girls, holding out to them his rites of ecstasy. But if I catch him under this roof, I will put a stop to him pounding his thyrsus and tossing his hair – by cutting his head from his body! 195

He is the one claiming to be the god Dionysus, that he was once sewn into the thigh of Zeus; he is the one who was burned up in the flames of lightning along with his mother, because she lied that Zeus was her lover. 200 Do such outrageous acts not deserve death by hanging, whoever this stranger is? But here is another miracle! I see the prophet Tiresias wearing the dappled fawnskin! And my mother's father – an utter laughing-stock, playing the bacchant with the fennel staff! I am ashamed, grandfather, to see you so empty-headed at your age. Shake off the ivy! Get rid of that thyrsus 205 in your hand, father of my mother!

You have persuaded him, Tiresias! You want to bring this new god to mankind so that you can make more money from augury and sacrifices! If you were not protected by the grey hair of old age, you would be sitting in chains among the bacchants for introducing debased rites; for where the 210 gleam of wine appears at women's feasts, I say that there is nothing healthy in the rites.

CHORUS Blasphemy! Stranger, have you no respect for the gods, and Cadmus who sowed the earth-born crop? You are the child of Echion; will you shame your family? 215

TIRESIAS When an intelligent man takes a strong basis for his arguments, it is no great effort to make a good speech. You have a smooth tongue, as though you were thinking clearly, but there is no sense in your words. A fine orator whose ability is based on confidence is a bad citizen, since he lacks good judgement. 220

This new god you ridicule – I cannot begin to tell you how great he will be in Greece. Young man, there are two things that come first for mankind: the goddess Demeter – she is the earth, but call her what you like – she nourishes mortals with food; the son of Semele came later, and he is Demeter's counterpart, since he discovered and gave to mortals a drink, the 225 juice of the grape. It puts an end to the pain of suffering humans, when they are filled with the stream of the vine, and it gives sleep to forget the troubles of the day; there is no other cure for pain. Itself a god, to the gods it is poured as a libation, so that through Dionysus people may have good fortune. 230

235–7 the ether This was the bright, shining matter surrounding the air of the atmosphere. It seems that gods could sculpt it into shapes which appeared solid (see 533–4), and Zeus did so to make Hera think Dionysus was dead.

Rationality and faith (231–9)

Tiresias' explanation of the 'thigh story' is etymological; the Greek for 'thigh' (*ho mēros*) is almost the same as the Greek for 'hostage' (*homēros*). Such theorising was popular with dramatists as well as with sophists.

● How consistent are Tiresias' views on sophistry?

240 also a prophet Tiresias lists further powers of Dionysus. Neither of these – prophecy and military influence – is a traditional part of Dionysiac worship, but perhaps Tiresias is trying to emphasise the breadth of the god's powers.

● Do you think Tiresias believes in Dionysus' powers? Or is he inventing far-fetched arguments to overwhelm or bamboozle Pentheus?

245–7 In time you will see him Tiresias makes a prophecy. Although his prophecy is unusual, he is right, as he always is (see note on page 10).

245 Delphi The oracle of Apollo at Delphi was the most famous in the ancient world. Tiresias connects the prophetic gifts of Apollo and Dionysus.

251–4 Dionysus will not compel Tiresias makes a strong point here. Dionysus will also point out that sex is not necessarily connected with his worship (398).

255–7 Tiresias points out that Pentheus and Dionysus are alike in seeking glorification.

● How far does Euripides make these cousins resemble one another? What traits do they have in common?

260–1 You are mad Tiresias reveals what he thinks of Pentheus' state of mind. He may mean that madness itself is agonising, feeling pity for Pentheus, or he may be thinking with fear of madness' painful consequences.

● Does Tiresias feel fear or pity (or both)?

● Do you think Tiresias has been treating Pentheus as though he were mad throughout this scene? How might he deliver his arguments?

262 you do not shame Phoebus Tiresias is the prophet of Phoebus (another name for Apollo). The Chorus mean that he represents his master well.

You pour scorn on him and the story that he was sewn into Zeus' thigh? I will explain to you what that really means. When Zeus snatched him from the lightning's fire and took the baby to Olympus as a god, Hera wanted to throw it out of heaven. But Zeus found a way to stop her, in a manner worthy of a god; he broke off a part of the ether that encircles the earth, and handed it over to her as a hostage, so saving Dionysus from the jealousy of Hera. In time, humans confused the words and made up the story that he was sewn up in Zeus' thigh, since the god was once a hostage to the goddess Hera.

This god is also a prophet, for that which is Bacchic and manic has great prophetic power; when the god enters fully into a mortal's body, he makes those who are possessed tell the future. He also shares a part of Ares' domain, for terror can scatter an army even when it is fully armed and arrayed for battle, before anyone touches a spear; this madness too comes from Dionysus. In time you will see him even on the cliffs of Delphi, leaping with pine torches over the twin-peaked plateau, swinging and brandishing the Bacchic branch, great throughout Greece.

Take my advice, Pentheus. Do not be too sure that force dominates mankind. If you have an opinion, and that opinion is weak, do not consider it wisdom. Accept the god in this country, and pour libations; become a bacchant, and garland your head. Dionysus will not compel women to be virtuous where Aphrodite is concerned; you must watch for that in their own nature, for even in the Bacchic celebrations a woman who has a sense of right will not be corrupted.

Think how you are delighted when crowds flock to your doors, and the city glorifies the name of Pentheus. So Dionysus, I believe, rejoices in being honoured and so I, and Cadmus whom you ridiculed, will crown ourselves with ivy, and we will dance. We are an aged pair, but we will dance nonetheless; I will not be persuaded by your words to fight with the gods. You are mad, agonisingly mad, and you will not be cured by drugs, although some drug must have caused your sickness.

CHORUS Old man, you do not shame Phoebus with your words,
and in honouring the great god Bromios you show wisdom.

264 Where we might have expected Pentheus to answer Tiresias, Cadmus intervenes, trying to strengthen Tiresias' argument.

Expediency

267 Tell a lie Characters expressing this kind of sentiment made Euripides notorious (at least in comic satire) for debasing the moral tone of tragedy. However, it has also been argued that this expansion of the tragic range was part of his genius. Certainly it is a vivid part of the characterisation of Cadmus.

● Do you see the inclusion of such anti-heroic themes as a strength or a weakness?

269–71 the grim fate of Actaeon In the usual version of the story, Actaeon angered Artemis accidentally by seeing her bathing. Euripides invents a version in which Actaeon's arrogance causes his *nemesis* (see note on 190).

● Why does he do this?

273 Take your hands off me! Pentheus is enraged by the suggestion; it sounds as though he pushes Cadmus away from him. He returns Tiresias' accusation of madness, and goes on to order a punishment that is particularly vindictive.

277 sacred fillets These fringes of white wool had several sacred connotations (see 96). They were hung from trees at places of religious importance.

279 track down the effeminate foreigner Pentheus commands the arrest of the stranger, now suggesting that he be stoned rather than decapitated.

● Is stoning a significantly different kind of punishment? Or is Pentheus just inconsistent in his fury?

283 You poor wretch Tiresias sounds sorrowful rather than angry; he even suggests praying to Dionysus on Pentheus' behalf.

● How does this make you feel towards Tiresias, towards Pentheus, and towards Dionysus, who has already promised to punish Pentheus?

289 Let Pentheus Pentheus' name is very similar to the Greek word *penthos*, meaning pain or grief. The connection will be made again in the play, to hint at future suffering.

290 I am not making a prophecy Tiresias is not using his art to see the future; he simply offers guidance on sensible behaviour.

○ Much of the impact of this scene arises from the gulf between the two sides. The old men and Pentheus are equally convinced of the other's folly, if not madness. Try staging the scene to reflect both standpoints. Focus also on the differences between Tiresias and Cadmus.

CADMUS My son, Tiresias has given you good advice. Your home must be with us, not outside our ways and traditions. Now your mind is up in the air, and your thinking is empty of thought. Even if this person is no god, as you say, declare him one! Tell a lie in a good cause: say that he is Semele's son, so that she may have the fame of mothering a god, and honour may come to our whole family. You know the grim fate of Actaeon, torn apart by the flesh-eating dogs he reared, for boasting that he was better than Artemis at hunting in the mountain glades. Do not suffer that fate! Here, I will crown your head with ivy; give honour to the god with us. 265 270

PENTHEUS Take your hands off me! Go and play the bacchant, but don't wipe your stupidity off on me! This man who taught you your folly I will punish. Go, someone, immediately to the seat where he practises his prophecy! Lever it up with crowbars and turn it upside-down! Throw everything into utter confusion, and hurl his sacred fillets to the whirling of the winds! That is how I will hurt him most. 275

Let others go through the city and track down the effeminate foreigner, who has brought a new disease to our women, and is dishonouring their beds. And if you catch him, bring him here in chains, to be punished by stoning and so die. It will be a bitter Bacchic festival he sees in Thebes! 280

TIRESIAS You poor wretch, how ignorant you are of what you are saying! You were not in your right mind before, and now you are raving.

Let us go, Cadmus, and beseech the god on behalf of this man, wild as he is, and on behalf of the city; beseech the god to take no action. Follow me with your ivy staff, and try to support me, and I will do the same for you. It is shameful for two old men to fall over; nonetheless, let us go. Bacchus, son of Zeus, must be served. Let Pentheus bring no pain upon your house, Cadmus. I am not making a prophecy, but stating facts; the fool is speaking folly. 285 290

FIRST CHORAL ODE (1ST *STASIMON*) (292–346)

Greek tragedy is formally structured, moving between Chorus and actors. After the *Parodos*, the action of the play is punctuated by five choral songs. The actors are usually all offstage, and music accompanies the singing dancers. The Chorus provide a variation in emotional intensity, and often give a new perspective on the conflicts of the action.

As the two old men leave the stage, the Chorus sing an ode to holiness. Unlike most Choruses, who are relatively neutral in their sympathies, these women vehemently condemn the arrogance of the young king Pentheus.

292 Holiness, queen of the gods In Greek thought, there is no hard line drawn between personified gods (like Zeus) and abstract ideas such as Holiness. Peace, Desire, War and Victory, for example, could also be regarded as divinities.

308–19 Unbridled mouths Extolling the virtues of a modest and respectful life is common in tragic choruses. The subject has particular importance in this play.

314 Wisdom is not cleverness Issues relating to thought and morality are often raised and debated in this play (see also 216–20, 399–400).

320 Let me go to Cyprus Choruses, who are usually citizens of the place where the play is set, often wish to be far away. There may be irony in the fact that these women are travellers who have only just arrived in Greece.

● Why did Euripides make his chorus foreign? What differences would it make to the play if they were Theban men or women?

Cyprus was the home of the *Erōtes*, personifications of love, and the birthplace of Aphrodite. Pentheus has already made it clear that he believes these 'bacchants' are worshipping Aphrodite (by having sex).

● Why are Dionysus and Aphrodite often associated?

324 Paphos is a city in Cyprus near Aphrodite's birthplace. **The hundred-mouthed… river… without rain** presents a problem; it is almost certainly the Nile, but it is nowhere near Cyprus (see map on page viii). It is possible that Paphos is a corruption of the original 'Pharos', an island near the mouth of the Nile. However, Pharos seems to have no relevance here.

There was an ancient belief that the Nile passed under the Mediterranean. Euripides may be alluding to an idea that it resurfaced in Paphos, just as the Greek river Alpheius was believed to resurface in Syracuse in Sicily (see map on page viii). This idea is unattested, but would make good sense of the text.

CHORUS   Holiness, queen of the gods,
Holiness, passing on golden wings
Across the face of the Earth,
Do you hear the words of Pentheus?   295
Do you hear his unholy insult
Against Bromios, son of Semele,
The first god of the blessed
At lovely-garlanded festivals?
This is what he ordains: 300
To join in dancing bands,
To laugh to the flute,
And to put an end to troubles
When the gleam of the grape is poured
At the feast of the gods,   305
And the wine bowl throws sleep over men
At festivals, crowned with ivy.

Unbridled mouths and lawless folly
End in disaster.
But the life of peace, and good sense,   310
Stays unshaken, holds houses together.
Though they dwell far away in the sky,
The heavenly ones see what mortals do.
Wisdom is not cleverness,
Or ideas beyond mortal limits.   315
Life is short; one who seeks greatness
Misses what lies at hand.
These are the ways of madmen, in my eyes,
Of people who cannot see sense.

Let me go to Cyprus,   320
The island of Aphrodite,
Where there dwell the Loves
Who enchant the minds of mortals;
To Paphos,
Which the hundred-mouthed stream of the foreign river   325
Makes fruitful without rain;

327 beautiful Pieria This lovely region on the northern side of Mount Olympus (see map on page viii) was the birthplace of the Muses, goddesses of song, dance, poetry and art. It is natural that the singing, dancing women would long to be there.

328 the holy slopes The gods lived on the peak of Olympus.

332 There are the Graces, there is Desire The Graces, goddesses of the arts, nature and beauty, had long been associated with Dionysus. Desire, or *Pothos*, was Aphrodite's son, often pictured playing a flute or drum.

336–46 The Chorus expound the way of life commended by Dionysus, and praise the virtues of simplicity, reverence, modesty, the pleasure of wine, and peace.

● How does this ode relate to the previous episode? How do the content and mood differ from the *Parodos*?

SECOND EPISODE (347–433)

An unnamed soldier begins the central section of the play. He appears on the stage escorting Dionysus, who wears the same smiling mask we saw at the beginning. The soldier makes a point of describing the gentleness of the stranger under arrest.

This episode contains the first of three confrontations between Pentheus and Dionysus.

347–8 we have captured the prey The imagery of hunting is crucial in the play, just as the references to Actaeon will become significant (see note on line 190). Although the soldier uses the animal metaphor in a jocular way, a pattern may be seen in Euripidean characters seeing the divine as animal. For example, in *Medea*, Jason describes the partly divine Medea as an animal. In *Bacchae*, Pentheus will confuse Dionysus with a bull (523–4 and 778–80).

351 I felt ashamed

● Why does the soldier feel ashamed? What effect might Dionysus' calm smile have on Pentheus as he listens?

354–9 So far, the god has not demonstrated his divine power directly, but the miraculous event described here will be the first of many.

● How do you think Pentheus reacts to the soldier's willingness to believe in miracles?

To beautiful Pieria, home of the Muses,
And the holy slopes of Olympus.
Take me there,
Bromios, Bromios!   330
Leader, god of joy!
There are the Graces, there is Desire;
There it is right for the bacchants to revel.

The god, the son of Zeus,
Delights in the feasts.   335
He loves Peace who grants plenty,
Goddess who looks after the young;
He gives the pleasure of wine that cures grief
To rich and poor alike;
But he hates the one who does not care for this –   340
By day and happy night to live to the end
The life of blessedness;
To keep his sense and wits intact
Away from 'superior' men.
Whatever simple folk consider right, and follow,   345
That I would accept.

SOLDIER Pentheus, here we are; our mission was not in vain, for we have
captured the prey you sent us after. But this wild beast was gentle to us, and
did not run away. He held out his hands quite willingly, and his pink cheeks
did not turn pale; he even smiled as he waited, allowing himself to be bound   350
and led away, making my job easy for me. I felt ashamed, and said: 'Stranger,
I am not arresting you because I want to; it was Pentheus who sent me with
these orders.'

As for those bacchants, the ones you had seized, shackled in chains and
locked up in the public prison – they are gone, set free, skipping away to the 355
mountain glades, calling to their god Bromios. The chains on their legs
snapped apart all by themselves, and the bolted gates opened without being
touched by any human hand. This man who has come to Thebes is full of
miracles. What to do next is up to you.

363–6 Pentheus is convinced that sex is central to the cult brought by this stranger.

Agon

An *agon* is a contest or trial. In drama, the word is used to refer to a dialogue of confrontation. The antagonists may attack and answer one another in long speeches, or, as here, in *stichomythia* – short, single-line crossfire. It is easy to misread such exchanges; bear in mind all the dramatic possibilities of pace and pauses. While the characters do answer one another, there may be deliberate discontinuities reflecting their different agendas.

○ Explore the possibilities of this encounter. Dionysus could be played in several ways, all different in their effect. Of course, his mask continues to smile, but he could be quiet or loud, playful or menacing, straightforward or sardonic. Consider what differences his tone might make to the sympathies of the audience.

○ Pentheus' character also leaves room for different interpretations. Is he hostile? Is he nervous or confident? Does he feel contempt for the stranger, or fascination?

373–5 Dionysus, son of Zeus On many occasions, Dionysus seems to enjoy speaking of himself in his replies, which seem like riddles to Pentheus. Here he takes the opportunity to assert his parentage.

379 What form Pentheus is curious about what these bacchants actually do; he has already expressed his suspicions.

380–3 It is forbidden... It is not permitted It was a central feature of mystery cults that the details could only be revealed to initiates.

● Is Dionysus simply stating facts? Or is he deliberately frustrating and tempting Pentheus, as the young king assumes?

PENTHEUS Let go of his arms! He is in my net, and he is not so quick that   360
he can get away from me.

Well, stranger, you are not bad-looking – to women, at least, which is
what you came to Thebes for. Your hair is long – you don't wrestle – curling
down to your cheeks; very seductive! You take care to keep your skin fair,
not exposing it to the rays of the sun, but keeping it in darkness when you   365
hunt Aphrodite with your beauty. So, tell me first who you are, and from
what people.

DIONYSUS It is nothing to boast of, and easy to tell you. I imagine
you have heard of Tmolus, where the flowers grow.

PENTHEUS I know it. It circles the city of Sardis.   370

DIONYSUS I am from there. Lydia is my homeland.

PENTHEUS How is it that you bring these rites to Hellas?

DIONYSUS Dionysus, son of Zeus, initiated me.

PENTHEUS There is some Zeus over there, who fathers new gods?

DIONYSUS No. He is the same Zeus who married Semele here.   375

PENTHEUS Was it in a dream, or face-to-face, that the god commanded
you?

DIONYSUS We saw each other face-to-face when he gave me his rites.

PENTHEUS What form do they take, these mysteries of yours?

DIONYSUS It is forbidden to tell those who are not initiated in the Bacchic   380
ways.

PENTHEUS What good do they do the worshippers?

384 to make me want to hear Whatever Dionysus' intention, Pentheus is certainly curious about the bacchants.

385–6 The mysteries… abhor a man If the stranger could really be put to death by Pentheus, this would be a dangerously aggressive remark to make.

387 You say you saw the god clearly
● Does Pentheus ignore the stranger's rather pointed remarks, or does he control his temper by taking a new tack?

The same thing seems to happen a moment later (391). Perhaps the emphasis is on Pentheus' curiosity, which will intensify dramatically at 679.

387 Pentheus imagines the 'real' appearance of Dionysus. Dionysus tells the truth; this play will show that the god can appear in many different forms. We have already seen him in human form; later he will appear as a bull (778–80).

391–2 Is this the first place This repeats information that Dionysus told us in the prologue, but it draws attention to the fact that we know more than Pentheus.

Barbarians
393 Because they have far less sense Greeks described non-Greek speakers as *barbarians* – people whose speech is a ba… ba… babble. More specifically, there was a Greek stereotype of Persians as uncivilised, effeminate and rather ridiculous.
● Do you think some Greeks in the audience might therefore side with Pentheus here? Or might these words in the mouth of such a character cause them to question such nationalistic stereotypes?

There may have been contemporary interest in the Persians as a result of the historian Herodotus' description of the people and their way of life. Perhaps tolerance might have grown with such interest.

399 You will pay the penalty As he grows angry, Pentheus cannot help throwing in a threat here. Immoral cleverness without wisdom is exactly what the Chorus and Tiresias have recently condemned as characterising the enemies of Dionysus. There is obvious irony in Pentheus using the very accusation which has just been made against him (see lines 216–20, 314–19).

400 *You* will pay Dionysus suddenly returns the threat. To Pentheus, who thinks he is talking to a man in his power, the threat seems absurd. Perhaps it has a darker ring for the audience, who are aware of Dionysus' divine powers.
● Certainly Pentheus is ignorant of the truth of the situation; but how irreverent is he? Does he see himself as irreligious?

DIONYSUS It is not permitted for you to hear; but it is worth knowing.

PENTHEUS That is a clever trick, to make me want to hear!

DIONYSUS The mysteries of the god abhor a man who lives without   385
reverence.

PENTHEUS You say you saw the god clearly. What was he like?

DIONYSUS Whatever he wanted. I had no control over it.

PENTHEUS Again you deflect the question and tell me nothing.

DIONYSUS One who speaks wisdom will seem foolish to the ignorant.   390

PENTHEUS Is this the first place you have brought your god?

DIONYSUS All of Persia now dances in these mysteries.

PENTHEUS Because they have far less sense than Greeks!

DIONYSUS No, they are right in this. Customs differ.

PENTHEUS Do you practise your worship at night or by day?   395

DIONYSUS Mostly at night. Darkness has sacred power.

PENTHEUS It has – to deceive and corrupt women!

DIONYSUS Even in daylight one can find debauchery.

PENTHEUS You will pay the penalty for your vile cleverness!

DIONYSUS *You* will pay, for your ignorance and irreverence to the god!   400

Divine mockery

402–3 Tell me Dionysus pretends to show fear, but the effect of his words is to mock the king who believes he has power over a god. Greek tragedy often represented kings tempted into *hubris* by their power over others.

In Sophocles' *Ajax*, Athene asks the maddened Ajax what terrible things he will do to Odysseus now that he has him in his power; in fact, Ajax has tied up a ram instead of Odysseus. Athene expects Odysseus to enjoy this mockery of his enemy, but Odysseus actually pities Ajax in his impotent madness.

404 I will cut off After the extreme threats earlier this might seem like bathos (a descent to the surprisingly trivial). However, the cutting of hair had ritual importance as part of a sacrifice.

○ It is possible that Pentheus does actually cut Dionysus' hair (presumably a wig) here, but it may be yet another unfulfilled threat. Which do you think would be more effective?

405 for the god Dionysus returns to riddles; he seems to enjoy referring to himself in this way. See also 409 and 412.

416 Seize him! Suddenly Pentheus hears one insult too many, and loses his temper. Perhaps this suggests that he was angry before, but keeping it under control.

● What is it about Dionysus' words or manner that makes Pentheus cut short the argument?

● Why does he say Dionysus is mocking Thebes as well as him?

421 You do not know We are reminded of Tiresias' words at 283–4. This also recalls a key moment in Sophocles' *Oedipus Tyrannus*. Tiresias accuses Oedipus of not knowing who he is.

PENTHEUS How bold the bacchant is, and most agile – with words!

DIONYSUS Tell me what I must suffer. What terrible things will you do to me?

PENTHEUS First I will cut off your lovely curls.

DIONYSUS My hair is sacred: I grow it long for the god.   405

PENTHEUS Next, give me that thyrsus in your hands.

DIONYSUS Take it yourself; it belongs to Dionysus.

PENTHEUS Then I will have you locked up and guarded inside.

DIONYSUS The god himself will free me, whenever I wish.

PENTHEUS You will be in prison with your bacchants when you call   410
on him.

DIONYSUS He is here now, and he sees what is happening to me.

PENTHEUS So where is he? He is not visible to *my* eyes.

DIONYSUS Where I am. But you have no reverence, so you do not
see him.   415

PENTHEUS Seize him! He is mocking me, and Thebes!

DIONYSUS I give clear warning to those whose minds are not clear: do
not bind me.

PENTHEUS But I say you shall be bound, and I have more authority
than you!   420

DIONYSUS You do not know what your life is, nor what you are doing,
nor who you are.

423 I am Pentheus Pentheus, angry and confused by Dionysus' words, reverts to the most basic facts. Perhaps he tries to assert his importance through his royal pedigree.

424 You are well named Dionysus refers to the painful connotations of Pentheus' name (see note on 289).

425–9 Take him! More threats from Pentheus.

● What did Pentheus threaten to do to the stranger if he caught him? Why has he not carried that threat out? Does his change of mind make us think more or less of him as a ruler?

The reference to the noise of drums may suggest that the Chorus have started drumming at this dramatic moment.

Staging the scene

● Who is in control in this power struggle? Does the balance of power change? What does the tone of the exchanges suggest about the physical action?

○ How would you stage the scene to highlight the emotions of the characters? How might the characters and Chorus stand in relation to each other?

SECOND CHORAL ODE (2ND *STASIMON*) (434–78)

The first *stasimon* followed the confrontation between Pentheus and the two old men. The first encounter between Pentheus and Dionysus is also followed by a choral interlude in which the Chorus develop the emotional content of the preceding scene.

○ The music and dance of the original performance would have been tremendously exciting. As you trace the emotions suggested by the Chorus' words, consider ways to heighten the excitement in your staging of the scene.

434 Holy River Dirce Dionysus mentioned this river when he arrived in Thebes at the beginning of the play. Acheloüs was the longest river in Greece, and therefore patriarch of Greek rivers.

439 Dithyrambus This word can mean a Dionysiac choral performance, a Dionysiac dancer, or Dionysus himself. Probably the first of these was the original meaning, and derives from *thriambos*, a triumphal song. 'Twice-born' was popularly but wrongly taken to be the origin of the word; such false etymology was common.

PENTHEUS I am Pentheus, son of Agave and my father, Echion!

DIONYSUS You are well named for disaster.

PENTHEUS Take him! Lock him up in the horse stables near the palace, so 425
he can contemplate shadows in the dark! Dance there!
    As for these women you have brought as accomplices in trouble-
making, I will sell them as slaves, or keep them as servants at my looms; that
will put a stop to this din of their hands, pounding at their drums!

DIONYSUS I am ready to go, but that which must not be, I cannot suffer. 430
Be sure, however, that Dionysus, whose presence you deny, will exact
recompense for your outrages against him; for when you wrong me, you are
imprisoning the god.

CHORUS   Holy River Dirce,
                        Blessed daughter of Acheloüs, 435
            You once received the son of Zeus in your streams,
            When his father snatched him from the divine fire,
                        And took him into his thigh.
                    He cried out: 'Come, Dithyrambus,
                        Come here into my male womb! 440
                I proclaim the name for Thebes to call you,
                        Bacchus!'
            But you, blessed Dirce, reject me when I come to you
            With my crowned bands of sacred worshippers.
                    Why do you refuse me? Why run away? 445
            I swear by the lovely clusters of Dionysus' vine,
            The time will come when you care about Bromios!

449–51 Pentheus, born of the earth After recounting the story of
Dionysus' birth (74–88), the Chorus describe the hardly less dramatic
origins of Pentheus (see Background to the story, page vii). They make
Pentheus sound like one of the monstrous Titans, also born of the earth,
who tried to overthrow the gods of Olympus. These women fear
Pentheus more than their leader does.

• Do their emotions affect our feelings about Pentheus and Dionysus?

456 my companions in worship

• Are these the same women who have been miraculously released, as
the soldier reported to Pentheus? Perhaps the women of the Chorus
have not fully taken in that news; they have not seen their escaped
companions.

463–71 The Chorus invoke Dionysus and list his haunts, as was normal
in Greek prayer. There is irony in this invocation as they do not know
their leader is the god. Furthermore, Dionysus is not in another country,
but inside the building before them.

464 Nysa This was a mountain sacred to Dionysus, but there were
several of that name. Probably it was the mountain in Thrace associated
with Dionysus in the story of Lycurgus. Lycurgus was an arrogant king
who refused to worship Dionysus. Dionysus sent him mad, so that he
killed his son. His people punished him by tying him to horses which
tore him apart.

466 Corycia was a cave on Parnassus, another mountain sacred to
Dionysus.

467 in the thick forests of Olympus Now that he is established as a
god, Dionysus might be found with the other gods on Olympus.

Orpheus (468–70)

Orpheus was a marvellous musician. When he played his lyre and sang,
wild animals and even trees came closer to hear his music. Orpheus is
grimly connected with Dionysus. After losing his wife Eurydice, he
wandered in the wilderness, half-mad with grief. There he accidentally
came upon a band of bacchants possessed by Dionysus. Taking him for
an enemy, they tore him to pieces.

471 Euios See note on line 121.

473–8 Axios… Lydias These are rivers in Macedonia (see map on page
viii), which the god would cross coming from Thrace to Pieria (327).
Lydias flowed by Aegae, the capital of Macedonia, where Euripides was
living when he wrote *Bacchae*. The geographical references have no great
relevance to Dionysus, and may be a compliment to Euripides' host
Archelaus, the king of Macedonia (see Background to the story, page
vii), who was also interested in horses and cavalry.

He rages, how he rages,
Pentheus, born of the earth,
Seed of the dragon, 450
The son of earth-born Echion!
A savage, unnatural creature, inhuman,
A giant so bloody he threatens the gods!
Soon, now, he will bind me in chains,
I who belong to Bromios! 455
Inside the palace he holds my companions in worship,
Hidden in the darkness of prison.
Dionysus, son of Zeus, do you see this,
Your prophets in the struggles of oppression?
Come down from Olympus, 460
Shaking your golden thyrsus,
And end the crimes of this murderous man!

Dionysus, do you carry your thyrsus
Leading the sacred bands on Nysa,
Home of wild creatures? 465
On the ridges of Corycia?
Or in the thick forests of Olympus,
Where Orpheus once played his lyre,
And gathered the trees to him with his music,
And gathered the wild beasts too. 470
Blessed Pieria, Euios honours you;
He will come to dance with his bacchants,
He will cross the swift-flowing Axios,
Bringing his maenads, whirling,
Over generous Lydias, father of rivers, 475
Who gives prosperity to mortals;
I have heard that his beautiful streams
Enrich the land of lovely horses.

THIRD EPISODE (479–727)

As though in answer to the Chorus' prayer, the palace is shaken by a violent earthquake, and Dionysus' voice is heard from within. He appears as before, as the human cult leader, and Pentheus comes looking for his prisoner. This is the second of their three meetings.

479 Io! This was a cry special to the worship of Dionysus.

481–2 What is this cry? The confused excitement of the bacchants is echoed later, when they hear Dionysus calling to them on the mountain. The dialogue is lyrical down to 508 – a musical metre appropriate to a scene of such emotional excitement.

Unseen voices

Cries heard from inside the stage building often mark moments of great excitement; indeed, many occur when a character is being murdered! (For example, Agamemnon in Aeschylus' *Agamemnon* and Medea's two sons in Euripides' *Medea*.) This scene is unusual in that the speaker is not the victim of violence, but its instigator; and in that he is also a god.

○ Is such unseen action more or less exciting than action visible on the stage?

492–3 Worship him! This passage is noteworthy because it suggests that members of the Chorus divided into two to speak the lines. Perhaps one half addressed and answered the other; or the Chorus leader may have given the command to the rest of the Chorus, who then responded.

Stage effects

● Did the original audience see the physical shattering of the palace building? Or is it described in such detail because it could not actually be shown?

Scholars are divided on this: some hold that such events would be too difficult to enact, and would be alien to the simplicity of the ancient stage; others think it would be easy enough to represent, and tremendously exciting theatre; still others suggest that the building would remain whole, but smoke and noise from the building could suggest an earthquake.

○ What do you think? Bear in mind what you know about the staging conventions of the Greek theatre.

| DIONYSUS | Io! Hear, hear my call! |
| (*from within*) | Io bacchants! Io bacchants! | 480 |

| CHORUS | What is this cry? Where is it from, |
| | The cry of Bacchus that calls me? |

| DIONYSUS | Io! Io! Again I cry! |
| | I, the son of Semele, son of Zeus! |

CHORUS	Io! Io! Lord, lord,	485
	Come now to our band of worshippers,
	Bromios! Bromios!

| DIONYSUS | Shake the floor of the world, spirit of earthquake! |

CHORUS	Ah, soon the palace of Pentheus
	Will be shaken apart and collapse!	490
	Dionysus is in the palace!
	Worship him!
	– Ah, we worship him!
	Can you see the stone lintels
	Above the pillar flying apart?	495
	Bromios is raising his cry inside the house!

| DIONYSUS | Set light to the bright blaze of lightning! |
| | Burn, burn the house of Pentheus! |

CHORUS	Ah! Ah!
	Do you not see the blaze of fire	500
	Around the sacred tomb of Semele?

508 And has turned it upside-down Compare this to Pentheus' earlier threat to turn Tiresias' sacred seat upside-down (275–6).

509 Dionysus reappears from the palace as the human cult leader, and the Chorus welcome him as their leader and protector. After the musically accompanied lyrical passage, the new section (509–43) is marked by an unusually light, lively metre.

512 Supreme light The women are overjoyed at their leader's escape; they are no more aware of his divinity than Pentheus is, but he is still their spiritual guide and the focus of their worship.

519 I freed myself
- What did Dionysus tell Pentheus when the king threatened him with imprisonment (408–9)?

The escape of Dionysus
This passage is in the form of a messenger speech (see note on page 40), but the messenger is also a major protagonist; the viewpoint of messengers is always worth considering.
- Study Dionysus' account of his escape. What features of his story strike you as important or strange?
- Consider how else a god might have escaped Pentheus' attempt to imprison him. What is the nature of Dionysus' divine power?

523 He found a bull Pentheus' delusion is most appropriate. Dionysus was particularly associated with bulls, and the Chorus described him as horned in the *Parodos* (85). Here Pentheus sees a bull as Dionysus; later he will see Dionysus as a bull (779–80). As Dionysus said (388), he could be whatever he wanted.

524–5 panting his rage
- Contrast the physical and mental states of Pentheus and Dionysus.

528–9 to bring him the river The way Pentheus gave his orders makes him sound comically confused. Dionysus seems to enjoy describing Pentheus' absurdity.

The flame she left when she was struck by lightning,
The thunderbolt of Zeus?
Throw your trembling bodies to the ground,
Maenads, to the ground!   505
For our lord, the son of Zeus,
Is attacking the palace,
And has turned it upside-down!

DIONYSUS Women of Asia, are you so stricken with terror that you have
fallen to the ground? You can feel the Bacchic god, it seems, shaking the   510
house of Pentheus apart. Stand up! Take courage and stop trembling!

CHORUS Supreme light of our ecstatic Bacchic worship! How happy I am
to see you after feeling so abandoned!

DIONYSUS Did you fall into despair when I was taken away? Did you think
that I would be thrown into Pentheus' dark dungeons?   515

CHORUS How could I not? Who would look after me, if you were to come
to harm? But how were you freed, after falling into the hands of that unholy
man?

DIONYSUS I freed myself, easily, without effort.

CHORUS Did he not tie your hands in binding knots?   520

DIONYSUS That is exactly how I humiliated him: when he thought he was
binding me, he did not touch or hold me, but was living on empty hopes.
He found a bull in the stables, the prison he took me to, and he tied knots
around its knees and hooves, panting his rage, his body dripping with sweat,
and biting his lips. I was close by, sitting peacefully and watching. It was at   525
this time that Bacchus came, and shook up the palace, and made the fire
blaze up on his mother's tomb. But when Pentheus saw it, thinking the
palace was on fire, he dashed this way and that, ordering his servants to
bring him the river Acheloüs. Every slave was put to work, but toiled for
nothing.   530

533 a phantom An ethereal Dionysus has been mentioned already in the play (235–6).

537 a most bitter sight This echoes Pentheus' earlier words to Tiresias (282), when he predicted that the stranger's revels would have a 'bitter' ending in humiliation and punishment.

539 to fight against a god This theme recurs again and again in the play.
- Do you think Pentheus is as mad or as irreligious as this makes him sound?

Humour and characterisation

543 Dionysus is in light enough mood to make a joke; he speaks of himself as a wise *man*, relishing the irony of his concealed identity. A lightness of tone and temper characterises Dionysus himself: he remains calm in the face of Pentheus' aggression, and wears a smiling mask throughout the play. There are notable points of similarity between him and his cousin Pentheus, but here is an absolute difference; lightness and humour are utterly foreign to Pentheus.

544 Pentheus comes back onstage, even angrier than on his first entrance. This is his second confrontation with Dionysus.

552 Who? Pentheus is still bewildered by events; note the number of questions he asks.

554 A line is missing from the text here.
- What might Pentheus have said?

556 I order Pentheus insists on giving more orders, even when his physical powers as king have been revealed as useless.
- Do you find him pitiful or laughable (or both)?

Pentheus abandoned this task, since I had escaped, and seizing a dark sword he ran into the palace. Then Bromios, I think this was just my impression – made a phantom in the courtyard. Pentheus rushed to attack it, and slashed the shimmering air as though he were killing me. That was not the only humiliation to which the Bacchic god subjected him: he shattered the palace to the ground. Everything is wrecked, and my imprisonment is a most bitter sight for him to behold. 535

Then Pentheus dropped his sword and lay down, exhausted by his exertions, for, though only a man, he dared to fight against a god.

Peacefully I came out of the palace to you, without sparing Pentheus a thought. I think – footsteps sound inside the house – he will soon come to the doors. What will he say about this? I will tolerate him easily, even if he comes breathing a storm, for a wise man keeps his good humour with his good sense. 540

PENTHEUS An outrage has been done to me! The foreigner has escaped me, the one who was imprisoned in chains just a short time ago. 545

Ah! This is the man! What is this? How can you be here in front of my house? How did you get outside?

DIONYSUS Stand still, calm down and relax.

PENTHEUS How did you escape your bonds and get outside?

DIONYSUS Did I not say that someone would free me – or did you not hear? 550

PENTHEUS Who? Everything you say to me is bizarre!

DIONYSUS He who raises the thick-clustered vine for mankind.

PENTHEUS   – – –

DIONYSUS You poured scorn on this blessing from Dionysus. 555

PENTHEUS I order the whole palace to be surrounded and barred!

Cleverness and wisdom

558–9 Clever you are, clever The Greek word is *sophos*, which can be used as praise or criticism, as 'clever' can in English (see note on Sophistry and rhetoric, page 14).

- What does Pentheus mean when he calls Dionysus 'clever'? And what does Dionysus mean in his reply?
- The nature of intelligence and wisdom is a key issue in this play. Look again at Tiresias' words on the subject (168–71, 216–20, 249–50) and the maxims of the Chorus (308–19, 343–6). Are they consistent?

560 he has come from the mountain

- How does Dionysus know where this man has been? Are the powers of the god becoming more obvious as the play goes on?

Messengers

The visible action of Greek tragedy was limited, partly by what could actually be represented on the stage, and partly by what convention accepted as proper. Generally speaking, attention was focused on the characters' response to unseen actions happening elsewhere in space or time. Messenger speeches were therefore part of the lifeblood of tragic action, pouring new events into the play, often of the most exciting or terrible kind.

This speech is central to the course of the play, crucial in the story it tells; but it also provides a kind of template for the second messenger speech from Cithaeron (902–78), which is the climax of the tragedy.

568–70 But I want to know whether

- Apart from the information he brings, what do you learn from the messenger's manner towards Pentheus? And what strikes you about Pentheus' reply?

570 excessively kinglike It is always worth remembering how much the audience, citizens of the Athenian democracy, prized their freedom from tyranny.

Bacchic rites (575–639)

- What impression do you form from the account of the messenger, a witness more impartial than the Chorus, Pentheus or Dionysus? How does it differ from the picture painted so vividly by Pentheus?

It is important to bear in mind that the women are not 'normal' bacchants like the Chorus; their state has been forced upon them. As Dionysus said, he has driven them out of their minds as well as out of their city. We cannot assume that all their behaviour is typical of Bacchic worship.

DIONYSUS Why? Can gods not pass even over walls?

PENTHEUS Clever you are, clever – except where you need to be clever!

DIONYSUS Where it matters most, there I am truly clever. But first listen to this man's story and learn something: he has come from the mountain to report to you. I will wait here, don't worry: I will not run away. 560

FIRST MESSENGER Pentheus, ruler of this land of Thebes, I have come from Cithaeron, where the gleaming falls of snow never melt.

PENTHEUS And what urgent message do you bring?

MESSENGER I have seen the sacred bacchants, whose fair bodies sped out of the city like spears in their frenzy. My lord, I have come wanting to tell you and the city what astonishing things they are doing, greater than miracles. But I want to know whether I can say freely what is going on there, or whether to censor my account; for I fear the swiftness of your moods, lord, and your temper, which is excessively kinglike. 565 ... 570

PENTHEUS Speak! You will not be harmed by me, no matter what; for one should not be angry with the innocent. But the more terrible things you tell me about the bacchants, the more will I punish this man, who has insinuated his arts into our women.

MESSENGER The grazing herds of cattle were just making their way to the upper slopes, when the sun sends out its rays to warm the earth. There I saw three bands of women: Autonoë led one of them, your mother Agave the second, and Ino the third. All were sleeping with their bodies relaxed, some leaning their backs against the greenery of a fir tree, some with their heads on oak leaves on the ground, carelessly, but decently; it is not as you say – that they are intoxicated by the wine-bowl and the sound of the flute, and hunt for the pleasure of Aphrodite in the secret places of the woods. 575 ... 580

Satyr assaulting a maenad. Dionysus (left) is holding a vine and drinking horn.

604–7 hunt Agave The confusion of normal roles, human/animal, male/female, civilised/wild, hunters/hunted, is one of the most important features of Dionysiac worship. Here, the men hunting women suddenly find themselves hunted, and Agave's cry at 613–14 (**my running hounds, we are being hunted**) stresses the ambiguity; hounds are not normally the prey!

This failed ambush of the bacchants will find a terrible echo later, in the second messenger speech from Mount Cithaeron (929–75).

609 Iacchus This was another of the cult names of Dionysus, particularly in Eleusis (just north of Athens), where he was associated with the Mysteries. The name was probably connected with the Greek word *iacchein*, 'to give a ritual cry'.

The Eleusinian Mysteries were a kind of fertility cult. Initiation involved swearing not to divulge the central mystery, which was probably veneration of an ear of corn symbolising the life of nature. Initiates believed that they were assured of a happy afterlife.

614 armed with the thyrsi This is not the first time that thyrsi are described as weapons (see line 19). It will not be the last (see lines 634–5).

When she heard the lowing of the horned cattle, your mother stood up in the middle of the bacchants, and gave the ritual cry, to stir their bodies from sleep. They brushed off deep sleep from their eyes and leaped up, a 585 marvel of decency and grace to behold, women young and old and still unmarried. First they let their hair down to their shoulders, and pulled up their fawnskins if they had undone the knots which fastened them, and they girdled the dappled skins with snakes that licked their cheeks. Some of them held a fawn in their arms, or the wild cubs of wolves, and they gave them 590 white milk, those who had recently given birth and whose breasts were swollen, having left their babies behind. On their heads they put garlands of ivy and oak and flowering bryony. One took up a thyrsus and struck it against a rock, and from the rock a dewy spring of water leaped out. Another struck her staff against the ground, and for her the god sent up a spring of 595 wine. Those who felt a desire for the white drink scraped the ground with their fingertips, and found gushes of milk, and from the ivied thyrsi dripped sweet streams of honey. If you had been there, the sight would have made you approach the god in prayer – the god you now deny.

We cowherds and shepherds gathered together and rivalled each other 600 in our stories of what amazing, yes, miraculous things they were doing. And one man who often comes to the city and is ready with words spoke to all of us: 'You who live on the holy slopes of the mountain, do you think we should hunt Agave, Pentheus' mother, out of the Bacchic dances, to please our lord?' 605

We thought it was a good suggestion, and we set an ambush, hiding ourselves in the foliage of the bushes.

At the appointed hour, the women began to move their thyrsi in the Bacchic dances, calling with one voice on Iacchus, son of Zeus, Bromios; the whole mountain, and the wild animals on it, joined in the dance, and 610 everything moved with their running. Agave happened to come near me in her leaping, and I jumped out of the ambush where I had been hiding, wanting to grab her. But she shouted out: 'Oh, my running hounds, we are being hunted by these men; follow me, follow armed with the thyrsi in your hands!' So we ran away and escaped being torn apart by the bacchants; but 615 they fell on the grazing cattle, with hands that held no weapons of steel.

Divine strength

Consider the deeds performed by the women, the power they not only feel, but demonstrate. Tiresias and Cadmus spoke of this divinely bestowed strength, and Pentheus will also soon feel it. Supernatural strength was associated with divine possession or madness in the ancient world, and even in modern times it is easy to find surprisingly similar stories. Such strength might be exhilarating to the person feeling it, but would be terrifying to anyone else.

627–8 There they turned everything upside-down We are reminded of what Pentheus did (or perhaps only threatened to do) to Tiresias' throne (275–6), and what Dionysus did to Pentheus' palace (506–8). This play is very much about normal life being turned upside-down under the influence of Dionysus.

632–6 The messenger describes a violent scene.

- What did Tiresias say (242–5) about Dionysus with respect to Ares, the god of war? Ares was also Dionysus' great-grandfather (see the family tree in Background to the story, page vii).

640 welcome this god The messenger is completely convinced by these miracles that Dionysus is a real god who commands their worship.

642–3 if wine ceased to exist Wine was regarded as a divine gift; interestingly, it seems relatively unimportant in the Bacchic rites described in this play.

- Why does the messenger mention Aphrodite here? (See notes on 194 and 320.) What effect would these final words have on Pentheus?

644–5 I am afraid Like the messenger, the Chorus fear the rage of the king; but they cannot contain their joy at hearing the miracles performed by their god.

648–51 Give the order Pentheus responds as he did when told of Dionysus' escape; he insists on trying to wield physical power, even when it has been shown to be useless.

- Is he foolish or bold? Can you find anything to admire in him?

648 the Gate of Electra This was to the south of the city, towards Mount Cithaeron (see note on Cithaeron, page 4).

You could see a woman pulling apart a young, full-uddered, bellowing heifer, with her bare hands, and others tearing fully grown cows to pieces. You could see ribs and a cloven hoof being hurled up and down. Parts hung dripping from the fir trees, smeared with blood. Bulls that were proud, with rage in their horns only moments before, fell to the ground, overpowered by the hands of countless young girls. The clothing of their flesh was pulled apart faster than you can blink your royal eyelids. 620

Like birds rising in flight, the women moved over the plains stretching below, which push up the Thebans' rich crops of corn by the water of Asopus; and then they fell like enemies on the villages of Hysiae and Erythrae, which lie on the lower slopes of Cithaeron. There they turned everything upside-down. They snatched children from their homes, and whatever they put on their shoulders stayed there without falling to the black earth, not even bronze or iron; and they carried fire in their hair without it burning them. 625 630

The inhabitants, enraged at being plundered by the bacchants, rushed to arms. Then there was a sight extraordinary to behold, my lord; for the men's spearpoints drew no blood, but the women, hurling thyrsi from their hands, wounded the men and made them turn and run – women overcoming men! Some god must have been there. 635

Then they went back to the place they set out from, to the same springs the god sent up for them, and washed off the blood, and the snakes' tongues cleaned the drops from their cheeks.

So, master, welcome this god to the city, whoever he is, for among the other ways he is great, they say – I have heard – it was he who gave man the vine that ends pain; if wine ceased to exist, then there is no more Aphrodite, no more pleasure of any sort for mankind. 640

CHORUS I am afraid to speak freely before the king, but still it must be said: Dionysus is as great as any of the gods! 645

PENTHEUS Already, close by, the wild outrages of the bacchants blaze up like fire; a terrible reproach to Greece. There must be no hesitation. You, go to the Gate of Electra. Give the order to muster to the heavy-armed soldiers,

Misogyny (651–2)

As with his xenophobia (see note on Barbarians, page 26), Pentheus'
hostility to the idea of women defying and defeating men would
probably have been shared by most or all of Euripides' audience. But one
role of the theatre, and of Dionysiac worship, may have been to
encourage people to overturn their everyday assumptions. This is
something Pentheus seems to find impossible.

● How much sympathy do you think the predominantly male audience
   had for Pentheus at this point?

Sacrifice (660)

The idea of a god demanding sacrifice is of great importance in this
play, as in several others by Euripides (see especially *Hippolytus*).
Euripidean gods require such worship, and when it is denied them they
can exact terrible revenge.

662 a great slaughter of women Pentheus is angry enough to talk of
human sacrifice, a gross distortion of worship in Greek eyes.

666–7 impossible stranger

● Why does Pentheus tolerate Dionysus' refusal to be quiet? How do
   you think he usually deals with contradiction?

His confession of perplexity in the face of Dionysus' intransigence leads
to a shift in tone. Dionysus takes advantage of Pentheus' bafflement and
seizes the initiative.

669 By taking orders It is worth noting that Pentheus regards his
subjects as slaves, and puts himself into a position where he cannot take
advice. The point would not have been lost on the democratic
Athenians. They cared not only about the justice of democracy, but also
about the practical advantages of debate amongst equals. It seems ironic
to us that these considerations did not seem to produce much debate on
the morality of keeping slaves.

and the riders of all the swift horses, and those who carry the light shield
and make the bowstring sing with their hands, for we are to march against   650
the bacchants! It has gone too far, if we are to suffer this at the hands of
women!

DIONYSUS You are not persuaded at all by my words, Pentheus. Although
I have been shamefully treated by you, nonetheless I tell you that you must
not take up arms against the god, but keep your peace. Bromios will not   655
allow you to move the bacchants from the mountains that echo to his sacred
cry.

PENTHEUS Do not lecture me! Since you have escaped your prison, keep
out of trouble. Otherwise I will restore your punishment.

DIONYSUS I would sacrifice to him instead of raging and kicking against   660
the goads, a mortal against a god.

PENTHEUS I will sacrifice a great slaughter of women, as they deserve,
creating havoc in the glades of Cithaeron!

DIONYSUS You will be made to run, all of you, and it will be a disgrace to
turn back your shields of beaten bronze before the thyrsi of the bacchants.   665

PENTHEUS I am quite ensnared by this impossible stranger! Whatever he
does or suffers, he will not be silent!

DIONYSUS My friend, it is still possible to put this right.

PENTHEUS How? By taking orders from my slaves?

DIONYSUS I will bring the women here without weapons.   670

PENTHEUS Oh no! This is some trick you are now plotting against me!

DIONYSUS What trick is there, if I wish to save you with my arts?

676 Bring out my armour Pentheus again loses patience with Dionysus' riddles, and starts to put the threat he made in 648 into practice.

677 Ah… At this moment, Dionysus suddenly switches his approach. Instead of cautioning Pentheus against his rash plan, he proposes an alternative.
○ How would you have Dionysus pronounce **Ah…** to attract Pentheus' attention? Questioningly? Imperiously? Beguilingly?

679 Very much! Pentheus cannot conceal his interest in seeing what the bacchants are doing; Dionysus comments wryly on the young king's sudden enthusiasm, and teases him on his inconsistency.
● Considering – as Dionysus points out – that he expects their behaviour to anger him, do you find Pentheus' psychology believable?

683 Not only does Pentheus confess his desire, he begins to imagine the scene.

688 Then you must Dionysus shifts from making suggestions to giving instructions as he takes charge of the situation.

689 What? Pentheus is startled by the nature of the instruction. He learns that he must dress as a woman, and a bacchant.
● If he is to stay out of sight whilst spying on the women, why does Dionysus tell him to dress up?

690 they will kill you Dionysus reveals the high stakes of the venture. Pentheus is risking not only ridicule.

691–2 How clever you are Now Pentheus appreciates the stranger's intelligence, because Dionysus seems to be helping rather than defying and confusing him.

PENTHEUS You have arranged this with them, so that you may practise your Bacchic rites for ever!

DIONYSUS I have indeed arranged it – that is right – but with the god.   675

PENTHEUS Bring out my armour – and you, stop talking!

DIONYSUS Ah... Would you like to see them sitting together in the mountains?

PENTHEUS Very much! I would give a countless pile of gold for it.

DIONYSUS Really? Have you fallen so passionately for the idea?   680

PENTHEUS I would not like to see them drunk.

DIONYSUS But still, you would enjoy seeing what makes you angry?

PENTHEUS Yes, sitting in silence under the pine trees.

DIONYSUS But they will track you down, even if you come in secret.

PENTHEUS Well, openly, then. That is a good point.   685

DIONYSUS So – shall I lead you? Will you undertake the journey?

PENTHEUS Lead on as fast as you can: I am chafing at your delay!

DIONYSUS Then you must clothe your body in a linen dress.

PENTHEUS What? Shall I change from man to woman?

DIONYSUS Yes, for they will kill you if you are seen there as a man.   690

PENTHEUS You are right again. How clever you are – and have been all along!

Transvestism and parody

Five years before this play, the comic playwright Aristophanes poked fun at Euripides in his comedy *Thesmophoriazusae*. In that play, an actor playing Euripides dresses his relative as a woman to go and spy on the women celebrating a religious festival. The comic transvestism is hilarious but unsuccessful; the relative is found out and captured by the women.

It is common to parody tragedy in comedy, but in *Bacchae* Euripides does something stranger; he takes Aristophanes' comic scene, and in a tragic context he makes it sinister. Pentheus' appearance in women's clothes, his madness and absurd vanity might well arouse laughter; but Dionysus' ambiguous words hint at danger which Pentheus does not see.

- Do you see humour in this scene? How many times does Pentheus change his mind? Is embarrassment the only emotion he feels at the prospect of wearing women's clothes?

706 you will spill blood Dionysus sounds another menacing note. Pentheus misses the point again.

Dionysus and the bacchants, American Repertory Theater production, 1998.

DIONYSUS Dionysus inspired me with these skills.

PENTHEUS So how should we put your good advice into practice?

DIONYSUS I will go into the palace with you and dress you myself.　695

PENTHEUS In what clothes? Women's? I am ashamed!

DIONYSUS Do you no longer want to watch the bacchants?

PENTHEUS Well... what clothes will you make me put on?

DIONYSUS I will hang long hair from your head.

PENTHEUS And the next item of my costume?　700

DIONYSUS A dress down to your feet. And there will be a headband on your head.

PENTHEUS Oh! And will you make me wear anything else besides that?

DIONYSUS A thyrsus in your hand, and a dappled fawnskin.

PENTHEUS I could not put on women's clothes!　705

DIONYSUS But you will spill blood if you make war on the bacchants.

PENTHEUS That is true. First I must go as a spy.

DIONYSUS At least it is wiser than hunting evil with evil.

PENTHEUS And how will I avoid being seen by the Thebans as I go through the city?　710

DIONYSUS We will take deserted streets. I will lead you.

712–13 Let us go inside... I will decide Pentheus still tries to insist on his authority as king, and the wry stranger goes along with the illusion.

715–6 I will go Pentheus makes a decision, but at once reveals doubt about what he will do. He leaves the stage, and seems not to hear what Dionysus says to the Chorus (and audience) before following him into the palace.

Threats (717–27)
At the beginning of the play, Dionysus told the audience that he would punish Pentheus and Thebes for refusing to give him due honour. Now he makes that threat very much more specific. Pentheus will not only incur the ridicule he so fears from the Thebans; he will go to his death.

The change in tone is sudden. After all his light teasing, the god (still, for the Chorus, in the form of their human leader) now promises death.

- Pentheus, of course, has threatened several times to kill the stranger. The characterisation is greatly affected by the conviction with which the two cousins make their threats. Which do we believe? How do we respond?

726–7 most terrible, and yet most gentle to mankind The neutral soldier described Dionysus as gentle at 348.

- What do you think of this self-description?

At 676, Pentheus was still threatening armed attack. By 717 Dionysus knows he has him in his power (**the man is moving into the net**).

- How has this come about? What are Pentheus' objections, and how does Dionysus overcome them? Consider how the dialogue reflects the shift in power between the two.
- How might Dionysus' physical behaviour demonstrate his increasing mastery of Pentheus? To what extent should the humour implicit in the scene be exploited?

THIRD CHORAL ODE (3RD *STASIMON*) (728–70)
This ode is structured in three parts: longing for the joy of free Bacchic worship; insistence that the ungodly are always punished; and thoughts on the origin of true happiness. The sections are separated by a repeated refrain on the nature of wisdom. The women of the Chorus sing an ode expressing their desire to escape the oppression of the city. They characterise themselves as a fawn (compare the foal at 141–2); in their simile, Pentheus is still the hunter.

- What is the effect of this, given Dionysus' last words?

The lyric metre is markedly lively and energetic. It seems likely that the Chorus here perform the Dionysiac dances they are singing about.

PENTHEUS Anything is better than the bacchants laughing at me. Let us go inside... I will decide what is best.

DIONYSUS So be it. Whatever you do, I am ready.

PENTHEUS I will go. Either I will go under arms, or I will follow your advice.   715

DIONYSUS Women, the man is moving into the net, and he will come to the bacchants, where he will be punished by death. Dionysus, the task is now in your hands, for you are not far away. Let us take vengeance on him! First, put him out of his mind, sending a lightheaded madness: in his right   720
mind he will never agree to wear women's clothing, but veering beyond the bounds of sanity he will put it on. I want him to be laughed at by the Thebans as he is led through the city disguised as a woman, after the threats that made him so frightening before! I will go to dress Pentheus in the fine clothes he will wear down to Hades, slaughtered by the hands of his mother.   725
He will come to know that Dionysus, son of Zeus, is fully a god: most terrible, and yet most gentle to mankind.

CHORUS   Shall I ever set my bare feet
To the nightlong Bacchic dances?
Flinging my head back in the dewy air,   730
Like a fawn playing in the green delights of a meadow
When it has escaped the terror of the hunt,
Beyond the stalkers and over the fine-woven nets,
And the shouting huntsman stretching his hounds
To the limits of their speed.   735
With great effort and flurries of running
It races over the flood-plain,
Rejoicing in the places empty of men,
And the green life of the shadowing forest.

740–3 What is wisdom? The nature of wisdom, *sophia*, has been raised several times in the play already (see notes on Sophistry and rhetoric, page 14, and Cleverness and wisdom, page 40). In this difficult passage, the ideas of knowledge and revenge are connected.

744–51 It is slow to move It is conventional in tragedy, and in Greek thought, that while the gods may take their time to punish the wicked, punishment is nonetheless inevitable. This concept was sometimes used ironically by Euripides; the wicked do go unpunished in some of his plays (especially *Medea* and *Orestes*).

● How many times has impending nemesis been foreshadowed?

752–7 a man must not think and act Like Tiresias, the Chorus make the point that reverence means being open and respectful to all manifestations of the divine. Although Dionysus is a new god, such reverence, they say, is an ancient tradition.

This draws together several themes of the play. Faith, for the Chorus, is wisdom; rationalism is irreverent cleverness.

762–3 the storm at sea Tragedy often uses the metaphor of danger at sea to highlight more personal struggles. Athens was a city very much dependent on the sea and ships, and the fear of storms would have been most immediate to the audience. The Chorus cite escaping a storm as an example of happiness, along with triumphing over hardship, becoming rich or powerful, and achieving hopes; but they seem to conclude that day-to-day happiness is best.

Peripeteia

The significance and relevance of this ode are debatable, but the dominant concepts are escape and revenge, crime and punishment, and the fickleness of human fortune. Although these ideas are not structured into a clear argument, they are very meaningful here at the centre of the play. *Peripeteia* was the term used by Aristotle to describe the turning-point, the reversal of fortune whereby the powerful protagonist becomes the victim. The themes raised by the Chorus here suggest that the *peripeteia* is happening now.

What is wisdom?   740
What god-given right is finer in men's eyes
Than to hold the hand of power over an enemy's head?
Honour is always precious.

It is slow to move, but nonetheless
Divine power is certain.   745
It corrects mortals who worship arrogance
And do not revere the divine,
Mad in their thinking.
In subtle ways the gods conceal
The long tread of time,   750
Hunting down the unholy man.
For a man must not think and act
Beyond the ways of tradition.
It costs little to accept that this is right,
Whatever divinity is,   755
And that which is held by tradition for ages
Exists naturally and for ever.

What is wisdom?
What god-given right is finer in men's eyes
Than to hold the hand of power over an enemy's head?   760
Honour is always precious.

Happy is the man
Who escapes the storm at sea and reaches harbour;
Happy is he who has passed beyond toils.
Each in his own way excels in prosperity and power.   765
Countless people have countless hopes.
Some end in prosperity for mortals,
And others pass away,
But he whose life is happy day by day,
He is the one I call blessed.   770

FOURTH EPISODE (771–837)

This is the third and final encounter between Pentheus and Dionysus. The balance of power has changed totally since their first meeting. Pentheus is now in the grip of the **lightheaded madness** sent by Dionysus (720).

771 You! Dionysus' words suggest that he comes out of the palace first, and calls Pentheus to follow him. He exclaims when Pentheus appears (776). The young king is wearing a long wig with the long robe and headband of a woman, and he carries a thyrsus.

Dionysus' tone is very like that of Athena in the first scene of Sophocles' *Ajax*, when she summons the mad hero from his tent and mocks him (see note on Divine mockery, page 28); it is worth reading that scene for comparison with this one.

● Are there differences in tone as well as similarities?

777–8 Now I seem to see two suns Pentheus develops double vision, and now sees Dionysus as a bull. This may be seen as part of his madness, or of his seeing more than he did before. The use of visual imagery is striking in this scene.

782 Now you see what you should see

● Why does he say that Pentheus sees as he should now?

783 But how do I look?

● What did Pentheus think about wearing women's clothes in the last episode? Has his disguise changed him?

785 I seem to see them Dionysus again humours Pentheus ironically.

787–8 I must have thrown it out of place Bacchants shook their heads wildly up and down as they danced. Pentheus is not just dressing as a bacchant; he has become caught up in the experience.

789 my job

● How does Dionysus portray himself? Why is it ironic?
○ Experiment with moving Dionysus to stand right by Pentheus, to adjust his disguise.

791 I am in your hands The Greek word *anakeimestha* (I depend on you/I am in your hands) suggests that Pentheus is not only guided by Dionysus, but dedicated to him – as a sacrifice!

DIONYSUS You! The man who desires to see what should not be seen, and seeks what should not be sought – Pentheus, I mean you! Come out in front of the palace and show yourself to me in the clothing of a woman, a mad woman, a bacchant! You who wish to spy on your mother and her companions!   775

Why, you could be one of Cadmus' daughters!

PENTHEUS Now I seem to see two suns, and a double city of Thebes, two cities with seven gates! And you – you look like a bull leading me, and horns seem to have grown from your head! Were you an animal before? Certainly you are a bull now!   780

DIONYSUS The god is with me now – he was not so friendly before. Now he is our ally. Now you see what you should see.

PENTHEUS But how do I look? Isn't the way I stand just like Ino, my aunt, or my mother Agave?

DIONYSUS I seem to see them when I look at you! But this curl has   785
fallen out of place. It isn't where I fastened it under your headband.

PENTHEUS I must have thrown it out of place when I was dancing as a bacchant inside the palace, shaking my head up and down.

DIONYSUS Well, my job is to look after you, so I will put it back in place. Keep your head still.   790

PENTHEUS Here, you arrange it: I am in your hands now.

DIONYSUS Your belt is loose, and the folds of your dress don't hang smoothly to your ankles.

PENTHEUS Yes, I think you're right about the right leg. But on this side the dress falls neatly to the heel.   795

DIONYSUS I am sure you will call me your best friend when you see the bacchants behaving more modestly than you expect.

803 *Stichomythia* (see note on *Agon*, page 24) can be used to debate an issue point by point; it can also be used to dramatise the lack of communication between two characters.

● Trace the discontinuities in this exchange.

798–9 Do I… hold the thyrsus There was no rule about holding the thyrsus; vase paintings show bacchants holding it in either hand. It seems that Pentheus is practising the way of moving described by Dionysus.

In the context of this scene, it seems likely that Dionysus is enjoying making Pentheus look ridiculous, and his words of congratulation underline the irony.

803–4 Am I not strong enough Like Cadmus and Tiresias earlier (153–7), Pentheus has the illusion of supernatural strength.

● Are there significant differences in their experiences?

809–10 See note on Divine mockery on page 28.

811 force must not be used to defeat women

● Is this consistent with Pentheus' attitude earlier in the play?

813 You will be hidden The Greek word *kruptō* (which gives us the English 'crypt') suggests not only hiding, but burial.

815–16 Pentheus still fails to catch the strong hint of menace, and returns to his obsession with sex (see note on 679).

817–18 that is just what you are going While Pentheus dwells on the image of what these women are doing in the bushes, Dionysus mockingly reminds him that his stated intention was to prevent such immorality. Again he hints at danger by suggesting that Pentheus may be caught first.

819–20 through the heart of Thebes Pentheus has quite forgotten his earlier fear of embarrassment at the thought of being seen in women's clothes. **Man enough** is ironic.

PENTHEUS Do I look more like a bacchant when I hold the thyrsus in my right hand, or in my left?

DIONYSUS You must hold it in your right hand, and lift it at the   800
same time as your right leg.
   I congratulate you on your change of mind!

PENTHEUS Am I not strong enough to lift the ridges of Mount Cithaeron on my shoulders, and the bacchants with them?

DIONYSUS You could, if you wished. Your perceptions were   805
confused before, but now your mind is as it should be.

PENTHEUS Should we take tools, crowbars? Or shall I tear up the mountain with my bare hands, putting my shoulder and arm to its crags?

DIONYSUS No! Do not destroy the homes of the nymphs, and the haunts where Pan plays his pipes!   810

PENTHEUS You are right; force must not be used to defeat women. I will hide myself among the pine trees.

DIONYSUS You will be hidden from human sight, as you must be, stealing up to spy upon the women.

PENTHEUS Ah yes, I imagine they are there now in the bushes, like birds   815
in the sweet clutches of love-making!

DIONYSUS Of course, that is just what you are going there to put a stop to! Perhaps you will catch them in the act – if you are not caught first.

PENTHEUS Escort me through the heart of Thebes, for I am the only Theban man enough to dare this deed.   820

821–3 You alone Dionysus' words are most ominous to the audience, if not to Pentheus. The god emphasises the isolation of the king from his people.

Encouraged by Dionysus' suggestion, the young king sees himself as champion of the city. He will indeed face a trial, but a more personal one.

● He takes Dionysus' words to refer to the fame he will win as a hero; what do you think he will be famous for?

827 You will be carried back The excited Pentheus takes this to refer to a glorious escort, a procession of citizens carrying him home. The truth will be horribly different – although Pentheus' mother will indeed carry him (see note on *Exodos*, page 72).

830 You insist on spoiling me There is a double meaning in the Greek word *trupha*, as in the English word 'spoil'; the ideas of luxury and harm are both raised.

833 Dionysus says that Pentheus is *deinos* – which can mean 'clever', but also 'terrible'. He seems to be saying that Pentheus is impressive, but in fact he means that Pentheus' fate will inspire terror because of its extremity.

834–5 There is a further double meaning in the Greek; Dionysus' first two words (*ektein' Agave* – **Stretch out… Agave**) could also mean 'Agave has killed…'. The meaning of the words is focused by the rest of the sentence, but the suggestion of death is ominous. Once again, Pentheus does not notice it.

Staging the scene

○ Consider how the change in the balance of power might be expressed on the stage. For example, would Dionysus seem more powerful standing quite still, or moving about, even circling Pentheus? And how might Pentheus' movements suggest his delusions of strength?
The tone of Dionysus' words is also of key importance. He could appear amused by Pentheus' state, seeming to enjoy mocking him; or there could be a hard, dangerous note to his voice, which Pentheus does not hear; or his tone could be quietly neutral, so that Pentheus and the audience interpret his sense very differently. Dionysus' smiling mask could echo or contrast strongly with his mood.

○ Try out the possibilities that the lines allow, and consider how they affect the emotional impact of the scene.

DIONYSUS You alone go to great pains for the city, quite alone, and so the trial you must undergo awaits you. Follow me. I myself will go to guide and protect you, but someone else will bring you back...

PENTHEUS My mother!

DIONYSUS ... as an example to all.   825

PENTHEUS That is why I am going.

DIONYSUS You will be carried back...

PENTHEUS Such luxury!

DIONYSUS ... in the arms of your mother.

PENTHEUS You insist on spoiling me!   830

DIONYSUS Such spoiling!

PENTHEUS I take what I deserve.

DIONYSUS You are a man to inspire terror, great terror, and it is to terrors that you go, so that your fame will reach heaven. Stretch out your arms, Agave, and you, her sisters, daughters of Cadmus! I am bringing this young   835 man to his great trial, and the winner will be myself, and Bromios. Events themselves will show the rest.

FOURTH CHORAL ODE (4TH *STASIMON*) (838–80)

The Chorus sing a song that calls for vengeance against their persecutor. The extreme violence of the tone is emphasised by dochmiacs, a powerful poetic rhythm.

Although the details of the imagined capture recall another earlier incident (706–7), the bacchants do in part describe what is about to happen to Pentheus.

838 swift hounds of Lyssa Lyssa is the personification of the madness which the gods send upon mortals, and which Dionysus has implanted in Pentheus (720). She is associated with the Erinyes, the immortal Furies who hunt down and punish those who have committed crimes against the gods.

846–51 As part of the events they pray for, the Chorus imagine Agave's words on seeing Pentheus. As in earlier choral lyrics, the repetition (**has come... has come**) may reflect the excitement of their chanting, but it may also have had a ritual importance.

849 Whose child Alleging doubtful or bestial parenthood was a common way of expressing horror and hatred, but here it is unusually ironic; who is the mother of the spy? The mention of lions will be picked up later.

852–6 As in the previous ode, the Chorus sing a refrain. The repetition (871–5) adds to the power of the invocation and reinforces the violence of the tone.

● How does the Chorus' idea of justice strike you?

Time

Most tragic action happens in real time, before the eyes of the audience (see the note on Pity and fear, page 84). Aristotle described this as one of the three tragic 'unities'; one event depicted in one place at one time. These were not rules, however; there are many plays where more time is called for. For example, in Aeschylus' *Agamemnon*, several weeks must be assumed to pass between the fall of Troy being signalled by a beacon, and the arrival of Agamemnon and his fleet.

As the Chorus sing this ode, several hours pass, during which Pentheus and Dionysus travel to Cithaeron, and the messenger returns to tell the story.

CHORUS   Go on, swift hounds of Lyssa, on to the mountain,
      Where Cadmus' daughters hold their sacred gathering!
          Sting them to madness   840
        Against the madman in women's clothing
         Who comes to spy on the bacchants!
       As he watches, his mother will see him first
          From a sheer cliff or crag,
         And she will call to the maenads: 845
    'Who is this man who has come to the mountain,
      Has come to the mountain, bacchants,
      Tracking the Cadmean mountain-dancers?
  Whose child is he? For he is not born of woman's blood;
         He is the child of a lioness,   850
       The offspring of Libyan Gorgons!'

          Let Justice appear!
         Let her come bearing a sword,
      Slaughtering with a stab through the throat
        The descendant of earth-born Echion,   855
       The enemy of gods, laws and justice!

      With unjust judgement and lawless anger
    Against your rites and the rites of your mother,
      With maddened spirit and frenzied intent
        He sets out to overcome by force   860
        That which cannot be conquered;
But death accepts no excuse for wisdom in divine affairs,
    And to live within the bounds of mortality
         Is to be free from grief.
  I do not hate intelligence; I delight in pursuing it.   865
      But other things are great and clear to see,
         And lead life to what is good:
  By day and into the night to do right and show reverence,
      To reject ways that lie outside of justice,
         And to honour the gods.   870

874–5 As in the second *stasimon*, the Chorus draw attention to Pentheus' own monstrous origins, and connect them to his crimes against the god.

876–7 Dionysus could take on the forms of wild animals, and Pentheus has seen him as a bull twice already; the Chorus are ironically unaware that Dionysus has appeared to them, as a man, without being recognised.

879–80 Again, the hunting metaphor twists and turns; Pentheus is both hunter and hunted.

FIFTH EPISODE (881–978)

The first messenger speech of the play, also from Cithaeron, was a magical tale, where both aspects of Dionysiac worship were revealed: the simplicity and pleasure of the worshippers at peace, and their terrible violence when threatened. This second speech also contains both aspects, but the violence is of a seriousness to eclipse the first altogether.

881 House and family It was common for tragic messengers to address the house as a personification of the ruling family.

883 How I grieve It is at once obvious that some disaster has happened, but not exactly what.

886 The Chorus immediately assume – correctly – that the bacchants are involved.

887 Pentheus… is dead Now, suddenly, we have confirmation of the event to which the whole play has been leading. The very simplicity of the statement is noteworthy.

Choral sympathy

The Chorus' reaction to the news could hardly be more striking. The announcement of the climactic event of the play, which is disastrous for the messenger and the royal house, is a cause for celebration for the Chorus.

- In many tragedies, the response of the Chorus to the action provides a model for the response of the audience. How does the reaction of this Chorus relate to your feelings as an audience? What effect does it have on your sympathies for the antagonistic characters of the play?

Let Justice appear!
Let her come bearing a sword,
Slaughtering with a stab through the throat
The descendant of earth-born Echion,
The enemy of gods, laws and justice!   875

Appear as a bull, or a many-headed serpent,
Or a fire-breathing lion for us to see!
Go, Bacchus, and with a smile on your face
Cast your net around this man who hunts bacchants,
So that he will fall under the deadly herd of maenads!   880

SECOND MESSENGER House and family that once had good fortune in Greece! House of old Cadmus from Sidon, who sowed in the ground the earth-born crop of the snake-dragon! How I grieve for you! I am only your slave, but even so, the great misfortunes of their masters still affect good slaves.   885

CHORUS   What is it? What news do you have of the bacchants?

MESSENGER Pentheus, the son of Echion, is dead.

CHORUS   Lord Bromios,
              You reveal yourself as a great god!

MESSENGER What's that? What are you saying? Woman, are you rejoicing   890
at my master's misfortunes?

CHORUS   I cry out in ecstasy,
                   I, a foreign woman,
                   In the music of Asia!
                   No longer I cower in fear of chains!   895

896 The messenger warns them that Thebes can punish them for their offensive rejoicing.

900–1 Tell me! Messengers always tell a story; usually, however, they deliver bad news to sympathetic hearers. Here, the Chorus are eager to hear about Dionysus' triumph over Pentheus.

907 so as to see Seeing and being seen, like hunting and being hunted, are opposites which may be confused under the influence of Dionysus (see note on 604–7). At this point, the women are unaware of their stalkers.

907–12 As in the speech of the first messenger from the mountain, the bacchants' world is idyllic when they are undisturbed.

912 Poor Pentheus Before anything has happened, the messenger reminds us that Pentheus is doomed. His sympathy for the dead king affects the tone of his tale considerably.

914–5 I cannot see This is a strange statement, since the messenger has already described the sight of the maenads.

- Is Pentheus' vision clear? (Remember that his sight has been distorted more than once in the play.) Or does he want a better view because he cannot see any 'shameful behaviour'?

Miracles (916)

This is not the first miracle in the play; the soldier and the first messenger both reported miracles (358–9, 567–8). It is noticeable that everyone but Pentheus recognises such events to be proof that a god is present.

MESSENGER Do you think that Thebes is so lacking in men...?

CHORUS   Dionysus, Dionysus is my master, not Thebes!

MESSENGER You must be forgiven, but there is nothing fine in exulting over crimes that have been committed.

CHORUS   Tell me! Explain how he died,   900
                The unjust man who committed injustice.

MESSENGER When we had left the houses of the land of Thebes, and crossed the streams of Asopus, we pressed on to the uplands of Cithaeron, Pentheus and I – for I was following my master – and the stranger, who was escorting our mission.   905

First, we settled ourselves in a grassy copse, keeping our movements and our tongues quiet, so as to see without being seen. There was a small valley surrounded by cliffs, with a stream running through it, and shaded by pines; and there the maenads were sitting, their hands engaged in pleasant tasks. Some were replacing ivy garlands on a thyrsus that had come unravelled,   910 and others, free as foals released from the painted yokes, were singing Bacchic songs in choruses that answered each other. Poor Pentheus, because he could not see the band of women, spoke up: 'Stranger, from where we are standing I cannot see these false maenads; but if I went up onto the cliffs and climbed a high fir, I would see their shameful behaviour clearly.'   915

Then I saw a miracle performed by the stranger: he took hold of the top branch of a fir, high as heaven, and pulled it down, down, down to the dark earth. It was curved like a bow, like a rounded wheel drawn with a compass, stretching its rim around; so the stranger drew the mountain fir down with his hands, and bent it to the earth, a deed no mortal could have performed.   920 Seating Pentheus on the branches of the fir, he let the young tree return to the vertical through his hands without shaking, careful not to let him be thrown. It towered straight up into the air with my master sitting at its top.

924–5 And instead of seeing Now is the moment when the hunt is reversed. Pentheus becomes the prey instead of the hunter.

925 the stranger was no longer to be seen Dionysus gives his command to the bacchants as an invisible god, as he did when he called from inside the shaking palace (see note on 481–2).

926–7 I bring you the man It is important that Dionysus describes Pentheus as a human enemy; the maddened bacchants will see him as both human and animal (946).

935 the speed of a dove Another strangely mixed image (compare 613–4, 624). Of course doves are fast, but they are also proverbially timid, the prey of other, fiercer birds. The idea of doves hunting is bizarre and striking; like Dionysus himself, they are both gentle and terrible.

938 they hurled stones at him Pentheus threatened to stone Dionysus (281–2); this is the first of his threats to be turned against him.

940 Again, as in the first messenger speech (634–5), the thyrsi become 'spears of ivy' (see also note on line 19).

Disguise and confusion

Euripides was always interested in the fallibility of human knowledge, and *Bacchae* highlights the problem most dramatically. Pentheus' downfall stems originally from his inability to recognise the god, and indeed even the Chorus fail to see that their human leader is also their god. The actual destruction of Pentheus is also a moment of both disguise and confusion. He is dressed as a woman, but not mistaken for one; Agave and the maddened women see him partly as a male spy, and partly as a wild animal.

944 Agave's leading role is emphasised (see also 935 and 951).

● Compare her words with how the Chorus imagined the scene in their last ode.

947–8 tore it out of the ground We see again the superhuman strength Dionysus gives his worshippers. That seemed a blessing to Tiresias and Cadmus, who were willing to follow the god; but it is not benign in the women who have been driven mad.

952 poor Agave The messenger injects another note of compassion at the point of greatest terror.

● Compare his sympathy for Agave with that shown for Pentheus (see note on 912).

956 my mistakes

● What mistakes is Pentheus acknowledging here?

And instead of seeing the maenads, he was seen by them; for just as he was coming up into their sight – and the stranger was no longer to be seen – from the upper air a voice, Dionysus, it would seem, cried out: 'Women, I bring you the man who makes a mockery of you and me and my rites! Now take vengeance on him!'

As these words were spoken, between the sky and the earth spread the light of divine fire. The sky fell silent, and the glade of the forest held its leaves still, and you could not hear the cry of any animal. The sound had not carried clearly to the women, and they stood up, and turned their gaze in all directions. Then he gave his command again; and when the daughters of Cadmus recognised clearly the order of the Bacchic god, they sprang off with the speed of a dove, running at full stretch, Pentheus' mother Agave and her sisters, and all the bacchants; and through the torrented glade and broken rocks they leaped, maddened by the inspiration of the god. And when they saw my master sitting in the fir, first they hurled stones at him with great force, climbing the cliff opposite, and fir branches were thrown at him like javelins. Others threw their thyrsi through the air at Pentheus, cruel target-practice. But they did not reach him. The poor man was seated higher even than their passion could reach, trapped and helpless. Finally they smashed off oak branches, and tried to rip up the roots with crowbars not made of iron. But when they achieved nothing with their efforts, Agave spoke out: 'Come, stand in a circle and take hold of the trunk, maenads, so that we can capture the climbing beast, and stop him reporting the secret dances of the god.' They put countless hands on the pine, and tore it out of the ground. Perched high as he was, from a great height was Pentheus hurled down, and he fell to the ground with scream after scream, for he realised he was close to his doom.

His mother was the first to start the killing, as priestess, and she fell upon him. He hurled the headband away from his hair, so that poor Agave would recognise him and not kill him, and he touched her cheek as he spoke to her: 'Mother, I am your son, Pentheus, the son you gave birth to in the house of Echion! Take pity on me, mother, and do not kill me, your son, for my mistakes!'

Violence

● The killing of Pentheus could hardly be more horrible. Does it affect
your overall sympathies in the play? If so, why?

Violence is frequently extreme in tragedy. In modern contexts such as
film, violence is often criticised as a cheap thrill that corrupts audiences
by habituation and trivialisation.

● Does Greek tragedy escape such charges by being classed as 'high art'?
● What purpose does violence serve in this play? Can you defend it?

973 rejoicing in her disastrous prey There is no longer any doubt
about who is hunter and who is prey. There is terrible pathos in Agave's
deluded delight.

977–8 The best thing Again the conventional maxim. Everyone in the
play except Pentheus echoes these feelings; the human problem is that to
know one's place and recognise the divine is far from simple.

Messenger speeches can seem long for modern audiences. In a
production of *Bacchae* at Cambridge in 1989, the events of this speech
were represented in silhouette behind screens as the messenger spoke.

● Do you think this is a good principle? Or would you keep the
presentation of the speech simple?

But she was foaming at the mouth and rolling her eyes in all directions, not in her right mind, possessed by the Bacchic god; and so Pentheus did not move her. Grabbing his left arm below the elbow, she put her foot against the wretched man's ribs and tore his shoulder out of its socket; she   960
did not do it by her own strength, but the god gave power to her hands. Ino was destroying the other side of his body, tearing his flesh, and Autonoë and the whole crowd of bacchants took hold of him. They all shouted out together, Pentheus screaming as long as he still had breath, and the bacchants howling in triumph. One of them was carrying a forearm, one a   965
foot with a sandal still on it; his ribs were laid bare by the tearing, and all the women, bloody-handed, were playing catch with the flesh of Pentheus.

The body lies scattered, one part under harsh rocks, another in the dense undergrowth of the forest, not easy to search out. His poor head happened to come into his mother's hands; she fixed it on the point of a   970
thyrsus as if it were the head of a mountain lion, and carried it right across Cithaeron, leaving her sisters in the dances of the maenads. She walks on, rejoicing in her disastrous prey, and comes within these walls, calling on the Bacchic god as her 'fellow-hunter, comrade in the kill, crowned in victory' – but through him she wins tears as her prize.   975

I will go now, out of disaster's way, before Agave arrives at the house. The best thing is to know one's place and revere the divine; I think that is also the wisest path for mortals to take.

FIFTH CHORAL ODE (5TH *STASIMON*) 979–96

In this short ode, the Chorus sing their delight at the triumph of
Dionysus over Pentheus. Their reaction is unusual. Other deaths in
tragedy are celebrated (Lycus in *Heracles*, the Egyptian sailors in *Helen*),
but the victims are unknown or wholly unsympathetic characters. The
nearest parallel is in *Medea*, when Medea rejoices in the news of the
royal deaths.

However wrongly Pentheus has acted, the contrast between the
messenger's sorrow and the Chorus' exultation might well produce
ambivalent feelings in the audience.

● Where do your sympathies lie at this point? How do you feel about
   the rejoicing Chorus?

EXODOS (a) (997–1054)

This was the name given to the final section of the play. Agave, Pentheus'
mother, appears on stage for the first time. She is still possessed by the
madness Dionysus imposed on her and her sisters as a punishment for
denying the truth of his birth. As with other cases of madness in tragedy,
the effect is most striking.

She is carrying her son's head. For it to be recognisable, it must be
either Pentheus' mask, or the mask attached to a dummy head. Either
way, the effect must have been grotesque. It is a visual completion of the
reversal of power in the play. Pentheus threatened to stone Dionysus,
and was stoned by the bacchants; he threatened to behead Dionysus, and
has now been beheaded at his mother's hands.

● What is Agave's dominant emotion? How is her madness reflected in
   her speech?
● The Chorus are exultant before she appears, but their tone seems to
   change as they speak to her. How? And why?

The metre suggests a macabre dance; perhaps Agave joins in.

○ How would you stage the scene to maximise its drama?

1000 a freshly cut tendril

● What do you think is the point of this image?

1002 I see it, and welcome you The women still seem to be celebrating
at this point, in a way that highlights the strangeness of the scene.

CHORUS	Let us dance to the Bacchic god!
	Let us shout out the disaster	980
	Of the seed of the dragon,
	Pentheus,
	Who put on women's clothes
	And the fennel staff made into a thyrsus,
	A promise of death,	985
	With a bull leading him to his fate.
	Cadmean bacchants,
	You have made your glorious song of victory
	Into a lamentation, into weeping.
	A fine accomplishment,	990
	To soak your hands until they drip
	With the blood of your child!

But I see Agave, Pentheus' mother,
Hurrying to the palace, her eyes rolling.
Welcome her to the dancing band   995
Of the god of ecstasy!

AGAVE   Bacchants from Asia...

CHORUS   What do you want of me?

AGAVE   From the mountains to the palace
             I bring a freshly cut tendril,   1000
             Prey that is blessed!

CHORUS   I see it, and welcome you
             As one of our band.

1004 without traps The fact that Agave has used no weapons in her kill adds to her triumph.

1005 This young cub of a wild lion Although she still sees him as an animal, Agave draws attention to the youth of her prey, and will do so again. There is further irony in that he is *her* 'cub'.

● Look back to 855, where the Chorus imagined Agave comparing and confusing humans and lions.

1008–10 As it did in Sophocles' *Oedipus* (see note on Cithaeron, page 4), the mountain almost takes on a personality for Agave.

1014 I am called 'blessed Agave' If this is true, it will not be so for long.

1018–19 after me Agave, like a proud hunter, is eager to claim the kill for herself; the irony is heavy.

Pace (1007–40)

The rapid exchange of dialogue in *stichomythia* always injects pace and excitement (see note on *Agon*, page 24). Here it is more extreme than usual; the speakers may even alternate between words, and the conversation is fractured and disorientating.

○ Try different ways of pacing the lines. Several times Agave seems to pause after a name, as if perhaps the sound of them begins to remind her of reality; the Chorus have to prompt her back to her deluded story.

AGAVE	I caught him without traps,	
	This young cub of a wild lion,	1005
	As you can see.	
CHORUS	In what lonely place?	
AGAVE	Cithaeron...	
CHORUS	Cithaeron?	
AGAVE	... killed him.	1010
CHORUS	Who was it who struck him down?	
AGAVE	That honour is mine first.	
	In the dancing bands	
	I am called 'blessed Agave'.	
CHORUS	Who else?	1015
AGAVE	It was Cadmus'...	
CHORUS	Cadmus?	
AGAVE	... Cadmus' daughters, after me,	
	After me laid hands on this creature;	
	This is a lucky prize!	1020

1021 There is a line missing in the text.

● What do you think the Chorus said?

1022 take your share Agave offers to share the spoils, as a successful hunter might, but the Chorus are shocked by the suggestion. Despite their recent rejoicing, they seem to feel the beginnings of pity for Agave now.

1024–6 He is young There may be absurdity in Agave seeing the youth of her prey without seeing who he is; but the effect is also moving. Euripides was not afraid to explore such complicated emotions.

1027 Yes, it looks like the hair of a wild animal

● How do you think the Chorus might express these words?

1028–9 Clever was the Bacchic hunter Again, the nature of intelligence is raised (see note on Cleverness and wisdom, page 40). Dionysus' mind is not in the mould of conventional wisdom; nor is Agave's judgement sound.

● What does she mean by 'cleverness' here?

1032 I praise you

● Are the Chorus still exulting over Pentheus' death? Why else might they mention his name here (1034)?

○ How might the Chorus speak these words, and how would you stage the scene to reflect the change in tone?

CHORUS	– – –
AGAVE	Then take your share of the feast.
CHORUS	What? I, take a share, poor woman?
AGAVE	He is young, this cub;
	His cheek is growing his first beard 1025
	Under the soft mane of his head.
CHORUS	Yes, it looks like the hair of a wild animal.
AGAVE	Clever was the Bacchic hunter, and cleverly
	He whipped his maenads against this beast!
CHORUS	Yes; our lord is a huntsman. 1030
AGAVE	Do you praise me?
CHORUS	I praise you.
AGAVE	Soon the Cadmeians...
CHORUS	And your son Pentheus...
AGAVE	... will praise his mother 1035
	For catching this lion-cub prey.

1037 Strange! The idea of Pentheus being called to praise her prey when he is the prey is bizarre even for the Chorus.

1039 Are you happy?
- Why do they ask this?

1040 I am overjoyed!
- What is the effect of this on you? And on the Chorus?

The Chorus' reaction
The lyric passage ends here.
- What has been the Chorus' reaction to Agave? Is it possible to chart their emotions through the dialogue?

This question is important because it is usual for the Chorus to guide the emotions of the audience in reaction to the events of a tragedy. Often their sympathies shift, especially in the face of human suffering. This play is unusual in how quickly and strongly these women have been affected between their exultation at Pentheus' fate and their encounter with his mother.

Location and dislocation
In most tragedies, the Chorus is composed of citizens, so that there is a feeling of public opinion. In this play, the people of Thebes are hardly represented at all.
- Why do you think this is?
- Which Thebans do appear?
- How important is the location of the play?

1047–8 with the white blades of our hands Once again, Agave is proud of having used no weapons (see note on 1004). Of course, it is relevant that Dionysus gave the bacchants the physical strength to commit the horrible killing.

Madness and laughter
1051–2 where is my son, Pentheus?
- What is the effect of this question when Agave is holding her son's head in her hands? Do you think anyone in the audience might laugh? What kind of laughter would it be? And would it lessen the feeling of horror?

Again, the madness scene in *Ajax* is useful for comparison.

CHORUS	Strange!
AGAVE	And strangely done!
CHORUS	Are you happy?
AGAVE	I am overjoyed!

1040

Great, great deeds have I achieved,
Deeds that are clear in this prize.

CHORUS Now, poor woman, show your prize of victory to the citizens, the prey that you have carried here.

AGAVE You who live in the fair-towered city of Thebes, come to see this   1045
prize! The beast which we, the daughters of Cadmus, have hunted down,
not with the thonged javelins of Thessaly, not with nets, but with the white
blades of our hands. After this, should huntsmen boast of their deeds,
needlessly buying the spearmakers' work? With our bare hands we caught
this beast and tore its limbs apart!   1050
    Where is my old father? Let him come to me! And where is my son
Pentheus? Let him place the rungs of jointed ladders against the walls of the
house, to nail to the beam-ends this lion's head, which I have taken in the
hunt and brought here!

EXODOS (b) (1055–1216)

There has been another lapse of time (see note on Time, page 62), during which Cadmus has been searching for Pentheus' body. Now he returns to the palace with the dismembered pieces of his grandson. The mood of this grim procession could hardly contrast more with the crazed joy of Agave.

Although certainty is difficult, it is probable that Cadmus would still be wearing the Bacchic clothes that Pentheus found so ridiculous earlier.

● What difference might they make to this scene?

1061–2 I turned back Cadmus had been to Cithaeron and returned already, and his phrasing suggests the weariness he feels; his earlier feelings of extraordinary strength have quite evaporated now.

1063 I saw Autonoë Cadmus remembers the fate of his other grandson, Actaeon, who was also torn to pieces on Cithaeron (see note on Cithaeron, page 4).

1068 the proudest claim possible There is more pathos in Agave's misplaced pride, contrasting so strongly with Cadmus' shock and grief.

1076 Oh, pain Cadmus says *O Penthos* – pain – the word that is so close to Pentheus' name.

1077–8 a fine sacrifice Sacrifice perverted is a common theme in Greek tragedy (see also note on Sacrifice, page 46). Pentheus was told by Dionysus to make a sacrifice, and Pentheus responded by threatening to sacrifice the bacchants. That threat has now turned back on him.

1080 with justice, yes Cadmus says that Dionysus has punished them justly, but too harshly (see note on 1170).

1082–3 If only Pentheus' own mother seems to imply that he was a poor huntsman.

● How does this affect your feelings for the dead king?

1085 Who will call him Again the horror is uncomfortably laughable. It wrenches a cry of grief from Cadmus.

1087–9 Cadmus is in an agonising position; he feels he must help Agave return to sanity, although that will mean causing her the most terrible pain.

CADMUS Follow me, carrying the pitiful burden of Pentheus; follow me,   1055
servants, to the front of the house. I bring his body here after the labour of
endless searching. I found it scattered through the ravines of Cithaeron,
never picking up two parts in the same place, as they lay in the forest that
hid them.

I heard of the terrible deeds of my daughters in the town, when I had   1060
returned within these walls with old Tiresias, back from the bacchants. I
turned back to the mountain, and I have brought home my boy, who died at
the hands of the maenads. I saw Autonoë, who bore Actaeon to Aristaeus,
and, with her, Ino; they were still stricken with madness in the woods, poor
women. But someone told me that Agave was coming here, with the stride   1065
of a bacchant, and I did not hear wrongly, for I see her now; she is not a
happy sight.

AGAVE Father, you can make the proudest claim possible: that you are the
father of by far the finest daughters in the world! I mean all of us, but
especially myself. I left the shuttles by my loom, and have come to   1070
something greater: hunting wild animals with my bare hands!

In my arms, as you can see, I am holding this trophy I have caught, so
that it can be hung on the walls of your palace. You, father, take it in your
hands; rejoice in my hunting, and invite our friends to a feast, for you are
blessed, blessed, that we have achieved such a deed!   1075

CADMUS Oh, pain that cannot be measured or looked upon! Murder is
what your wretched hands have achieved! You have struck down a fine
sacrifice to the gods – and you invite Thebes and me to a feast! Ah, I feel
grief for your misfortunes, and for mine too. The god, lord Bromios, who
was born in our family, has destroyed us; with justice, yes, but excessively   1080
hard.

AGAVE How bad-tempered people become in their scowling old age! If
only my son were as successful in the chase as his mother, when he goes
hunting wild animals with the young men of Thebes! But he is only able to
fight gods! You must rebuke him, father. Who will call him into my sight, to   1085
see how fortunate I am?

CADMUS Oh no! No! If you come to understand what you have done, you
will feel terrible pain; but if you remain in the state you are in for ever, you
will think nothing is wrong when in truth nothing is right.

1091–1110 It is perhaps not so difficult to show a character who is mad; but a plausible return to sense is a delicate dramatic challenge.

● How well do you think Cadmus manages Agave? How well does Euripides manage them both?

1094 It is brighter than before Just as the delusions Dionysus gave Pentheus affected his vision, so Agave's sight changes as she begins to return to reality.

1095 soaring excitement Cadmus knows that madness can feel exhilarating to the sufferer; he himself felt miraculously strong when he set out to dance.

1100 Agave is suddenly returned to a plaintive and respectful normality.

1101 Cadmus begins to explain what has happened by making Agave recollect the important facts of her past.

Agave with the head of Pentheus, American Repertory Theater production, 1998.

1105 Whose head Now he links Agave's returning memory and consciousness to her terrible present.

1106 For some time now, Agave has been convinced her prey is a lion cub. Just as earlier, when doves were surprising hunters (935), a lion is an unusual prey; but the truth is even more unusual – and horrible.

AGAVE What is wrong in this? Where is the pain?   1090

CADMUS First turn your eyes to the sky above us.

AGAVE Yes; why do you tell me to look at it?

CADMUS Is it the same, or does it seem to you to be changing?

AGAVE It is brighter than before, and clearer.

CADMUS And do you feel that same soaring excitement in your   1095
heart?

AGAVE I don't know what you mean, but I am somehow returning to my
senses. My mind is changed from before.

CADMUS Can you listen to me, and give me a clear answer?

AGAVE Yes – I have forgotten what we were saying before, father.   1100

CADMUS To what house did you go when you were married?

AGAVE You gave me to one of the Sown Men, as they call them; to Echion.

CADMUS And what son was born to your husband in that house?

AGAVE Pentheus, from my union with his father.

CADMUS Whose head, then, are you holding in your hands?   1105

AGAVE A lion's – that is what they said in the hunt.

CADMUS Now look properly; it is only a moment's effort.

1110 I am lost! Agave realises the first part of her misery – her son is dead. The realisation that she herself killed him is still to come.

1112 the head of Pentheus With her sanity and true vision restored, the head Agave is carrying looks nothing like a lion.

1115 Cruel truth Cadmus can hardly bear to make this second revelation to her.

1116 Tell me! Agave knows that Cadmus will tell her nothing good, but she is driven to hear the conclusion of her horror. The emotion is perhaps not so far away from what the audience of a tragedy might feel: desire to know the terrible conclusion.

Pity and fear

Aristotle was interested in exploring the construction and effects of tragedy. He considered the definitive tragic emotions to be pity and fear; pity for the suffering of the characters, and fear of their inevitable disaster. He particularly admired Sophocles' *Oedipus*, where the disaster is not an event as such, but Oedipus' realisation of the horror he has unwittingly caused. Euripides equals Sophocles here in Agave's terrible realisation.

● For which characters have pity and fear been evoked in this play?

1117 You killed him Cadmus tells her the awful truth as simply as he can.

1119 Where once the hounds tore Actaeon apart Once again we are reminded of the echoes of disaster linking this family and Cithaeron.

1121 He was going to mock Despite his grief, Cadmus is clear-sighted and honest about Pentheus' actions.

1125–7 Dionysus destroyed us Agave views the event simply, but Cadmus does see reason in the god's punishment.

AGAVE Oh! What am I looking at? What's this I'm carrying in my hands?

CADMUS Look hard at it, and understand more clearly.

AGAVE I see the most terrible pain; I am lost!   1110

CADMUS Does it look like a lion to you?

AGAVE No; I am holding the head of Pentheus. I am lost!

CADMUS Yes, and he was mourned before you recognised him.

AGAVE Who killed him? How did he come into my hands?

CADMUS Cruel truth, how ill-timed your revelations are!   1115

AGAVE Tell me! My heart is pounding at what is to come.

CADMUS You killed him, you and your sisters.

AGAVE Where did he die? At home – or where?

CADMUS Where once the hounds tore Actaeon apart.

AGAVE Why did he go to Cithaeron, the ill-fated man?   1120

CADMUS He was going to mock the god and your Bacchic rites.

AGAVE And we – how did we get there?

CADMUS You were mad; the whole city was possessed with
Bacchic frenzy.

AGAVE Dionysus destroyed us; now I understand.   1125

CADMUS Yes, for he was insulted, outraged; because you did not consider
him a god.

1130 Are all his limbs joined Agave has realised that Pentheus has been torn to pieces.

1131 Here there is another missing line.

- Suppose Cadmus said nothing. How might his silence be made expressive?

Cadmus' lament

Cadmus mourns the ruin of his house, his own fall from greatness to misery, and the loss of his grandson.

Cadmus himself is of key importance in this play. Initially, he was praised by Dionysus, and he was ready to dance for the god; but apart from cutting a rather ridiculous figure, he was startlingly cynical in his reasons for proclaiming the divinity of Dionysus. In his misery at the end, he draws sympathy even from the Chorus, but his fond reminiscence of Pentheus' reign of terror sounds an uneasy note. Perhaps they were both 'excessively kinglike' (570).

- Is Cadmus a powerful tragic figure, or a ridiculous and cynical old politician? Perhaps he is both; Euripides was famous (and notorious) for introducing heroes with strikingly human weaknesses.
- Do you regard Cadmus as the emotional focus of the tragedy, as opposed to Pentheus or Agave?

1138 you were the terror Cadmus says this with pride, although the Thebans might have felt differently. Euripides frequently explores complex or conflicting emotions.

1140 into exile Exile was a disaster for the Greeks; it meant the loss of home, family, friends, respect and security. Exiles were at the mercy of foreigners and fate, doomed to wander for ever in poverty and fear.

It is not clear why Cadmus must go into exile: he has committed no crime. Perhaps he is so shamed by his family's crime and punishment that he feels implicated, or polluted in the religious sense – tainted by his proximity to such a crime, and in need of purification.

1141–2 the great Cadmus As is common in tragedy, part of the pathos stems from the magnitude of the fall from greatness to ruin (see note on *Peripeteia*, page 54).

1147 Tell me, so that I can punish Again there is irony in Cadmus grieving for Pentheus in a way that reminds us of an unpleasant side to his grandson's life. On the other hand, the memory of Pentheus calling Cadmus 'grandfather' is moving. Pentheus was not only a king: he was a young member of this unfortunate family.

1152–3 I grieve Just as the Chorus felt sympathy in the face of Agave's suffering, they pity Cadmus; but they repeat the point that Pentheus deserved to die.

AGAVE And the dear body of my son, father – where is it?

CADMUS I found it with difficulty, and have brought it here.

AGAVE Are all his limbs joined decently together?   1130

CADMUS – – –

AGAVE How was Pentheus involved in my madness?

CADMUS He was like you; he did not revere the god. That is why the god joined you all together in the same suffering, you and your sisters, and him here, destroying the house and me with it; I have no male children of my   1135 own, and now I see this young shoot of your womb, poor woman, most shamefully and terribly killed. Through him the house saw light again; you, boy, son of my daughter, you held my palace together; you were the terror of the city. No one who saw you would disrespect me in my old age, for you would have punished him as he deserved. But now I will go into exile,   1140 without honour, the great Cadmus, who sowed the race of Thebans and reaped the fairest harvest.

Dearest of men – for though you are no longer alive, still you will be counted among those I love most, child – no longer will you touch my beard with your hand, and embrace me, calling me grandfather, and saying: 1145 'Who is wronging you, old man? Who is treating you with disrespect? Who is troubling your heart by being unpleasant? Tell me, so that I can punish the man who is wronging you, grandfather.'

But now I am in misery, and you have met a terrible fate; your mother is to be pitied, and your family suffers too. If anyone despises divinity, let him   1150 look on this man's death, and believe in the gods!

CHORUS I grieve for your fate, Cadmus, but your grandson has received the punishment he deserved, painful as it is for you.

1155 Here there is a large gap in the text during which Agave might ask to prepare Pentheus' body for burial. We cannot tell exactly when or how Dionysus reappears – probably as a *deus ex machina* on the roof of the palace or above it, suspended on the *mēchanē* (crane).

1156 As gods often do at the end of a tragedy, Dionysus foretells the aftermath of the events we have witnessed. As Tiresias said earlier (240–2), Dionysus has the gift of prophecy. The future he describes is as bizarre and terrifying as the fate of Pentheus.

Euripides' taste for tying up details of myth and history often shows at the end of his plays. There was a strong contemporary interest in aetiology (explaining the origin of beliefs and traditions), accentuated by the Sophists and the growth of local history.

1156 You will be turned into a serpent This is not attested elsewhere. Euripides may have invented it to account for an early tradition of worshipping Cadmus in the form of a snake as protector of house or palace.

1158 though you were only a mortal There is a suggestion that Cadmus' fate is due to having lived beyond the mortal limits recommended so often by the Chorus (he saved Zeus, married a goddess and founded a city).

1159–60 You will sack This might seem to be a reference to Xerxes' invasion of Greece in 480–79 BC. The Persian king destroyed many Greek cities (including Athens), and the famous shrine of Apollo (Loxias) at Delphi, before he was eventually defeated, and struggled home with disastrous losses. Herodotus (9.42) says that the Persians believed that Dionysus' prophecy referred to them; but he explains (5.61) that it actually referred to a tribe of Illyria, the Encheleis (Eels). When Thebes fell to the sons of the Seven, the Thebans joined the Encheleis to counter-attack their Greek home.

Despite Herodotus' opinion, however, Euripides may have intended Dionysus' prophecy to bring the Persian invasion to mind.

1162–3 the Land of the Blessed Although all mortals went to the Underworld after death, a few heroes went to a happier part of it. Cadmus does not seem consoled by this good fortune.

1168 You are late Knowledge coming too late is a frequent theme in tragedy. Aeschylus' *Oresteia* famously expressed the idea that learning – *mathos* – only comes through suffering – *pathos*.

1170 you punish too severely Cadmus dares to voice his feelings.

- Cadmus is impressively forceful; has he acquired this strength, or was this part of his character concealed when he first appeared?

AGAVE Father, since you see how my fortunes have been reversed...

– – –

1155

DIONYSUS – – – You will be turned into a serpent, and your wife will take on the savage form of a snake – Harmony, the daughter of Ares, whom you married though you were only a mortal. With your wife, as the oracle of Zeus proclaims, you will drive an ox-cart, leading a barbarian horde. You will sack many cities with your uncountable army, but when they have destroyed the oracle of Loxias, their return home will be wretched. But Ares will save you and Harmony, and give you a new life in the Land of the Blessed.

1160

    I do not speak as the son of a mortal father; I speak as Dionysus, son of Zeus! If you had understood what wisdom was when you rejected it, you would have had good fortune with the son of Zeus as your ally.

1165

CADMUS Dionysus, we beg you – we have done wrong!

DIONYSUS You are late in recognising me; when you should have seen me, you did not.

CADMUS We have come to understand that, but you punish too severely!

1170

Justice (1171)
Dionysus claims that he has acted rightly.

- Do you agree that the punishment of Pentheus was justified? Was it excessive? Cadmus seemed to suggest that it was both (1080–1).
- How does this question affect your emotional response to the play as a whole, to the dead Pentheus, and to Dionysus himself?

1172 It is not right Euripidean characters often voice the thought that the gods ought to be better than humans, but they are always speaking in vain. Dionysus, like Pentheus, liked to be honoured; time and again, it turns out that the chief difference between mortals and gods is one of power.

1174 Zeus agreed to this Dionysus does not answer the complaint, but simply refers to the authority of Zeus. Perhaps this is a way of saying that it has all been an inescapable fact of life.

- Is Dionysus morally evasive?

1178 My child, what a terrible fate Cadmus turns away from Dionysus to his daughter, and neither of them addresses the god again. Dionysus will do nothing for them, and their contact is at an end.

Dionysus foretold that Cadmus would ultimately find peace in the Land of the Blessed, but Cadmus sees nothing to look forward to. Gods and humans do not always share the same idea of reward, just as they differ on punishment.

1182 my wife, Harmony It is interesting that she plays no part in the play. Her first mention is at line 1157.

1185 Acheron This was the great river that flowed down into Hades.

1186 I will be in exile Agave will also be a defenceless exile, but it seems that her fate does not even merit prediction. It is possible that Dionysus prophesied her future in the missing section.

1187–8 like a swan Swans proverbially cared for their parents; perhaps their other legendary peculiarity of singing before they die is also relevant here. It is the last of the bird images applied to Agave and the bacchants (see 624 and 935).

1191 Here Agave breaks into song; the final section is lyrical to mark the emotional climax of the play.

DIONYSUS Yes, for I am a god, and I was insulted by you.

CADMUS It is not right that the gods should resemble mortals in their passions.

DIONYSUS My father Zeus agreed to this long ago.

AGAVE Oh, my old father, it has been decided; we are miserable exiles!   1175

DIONYSUS So why do you delay what is inevitable?

CADMUS My child, what a terrible fate we have come to, all of us: you, poor woman, and your sisters, and myself, wretched as I am. As an old immigrant I will arrive among foreigners, and there still awaits me the god-   1180
given decree, that I will lead an army of mixed races to Greece. And I will lead my wife, Harmony, the daughter of Ares, in the form of a savage serpent, as a serpent myself, leading the spear-carriers against Greek altars and tombs. I will have no rest from my suffering, and I will not sail down the cataract of Acheron and be at peace!   1185

AGAVE Father, I will be in exile without you.

CADMUS Why do you throw your arms around me, poor child, like a swan protecting its weak, white-feathered parent?

AGAVE Where can I turn, cast out of my fatherland?

CADMUS I do not know, child; your father is of little help.   1190

AGAVE   Goodbye, palace! Goodbye, city of my father!
                          In misfortune I leave you,
                          An exile from my home.

CADMUS   Go, child, to Aristaeus'...

1195 Another gap. Perhaps Cadmus suggests that Agave should seek help from Aristaeus, her brother-in-law, but this is of little comfort to Agave.

1200 brutality Agave describes Dionysus' actions in powerful terms; it is worth remembering that Dionysus described himself as terrible as well as gentle (726–7).

1201–2 After playing no part in the preceding exchanges, Dionysus suddenly speaks in his own justification. It is striking that the god can be so ignored by the human characters.

● Some editors read these as Cadmus' words, and propose that Dionysus left the scene after 1177. Which interpretation do you prefer?

1203 Farewell As in the English 'goodbye' and 'farewell', the Greek implies a hope for the other's happiness. Cadmus feels the irony of his own words in their irrelevance to Agave's misery.

1206 Lead me It is almost as though Agave is blind, after all her changes of vision. Her equally guilty sisters will go into exile with her.

1210 nothing to remind me of a thyrsus Dionysus' punishment has not made Agave eager to serve him further.

○ If you were staging the play, what feelings would you want the audience to have at the end? How would you stage the final section to achieve your aim? Would Dionysus remain onstage to the end? When, and how, might he go off?

Choral epilogue

There was no curtain in the Theatre of Dionysus, so these were traditional lines to make it clear that the play was over. In this play, the words do have some relevance to the problems of understanding between humans and gods, but perhaps the most important function of the words is to draw together the humans in the audience after their dramatic experience of the terror of divine punishment.

Roman Mosaic showing the young Bacchus.

AGAVE   I mourn for you, father...

CADMUS   And I for you, my child,
And I weep for your sisters too.

AGAVE   ... for terribly has lord Dionysus
Brought this brutality to your house.   1200

DIONYSUS   Yes, for your behaviour towards me was terrible,
When my name was without honour in Thebes.

AGAVE   Farewell, father!

CADMUS   Farewell, poor daughter,
Though it would be hard for you to fare well.   1205

AGAVE   Lead me, escorts, to where I can take
My pitiable sisters with me into exile.
Let me go where foul Cithaeron cannot see me,
Where my eyes cannot see Cithaeron,
Where there is nothing to remind me of a thyrsus.   1210
Leave them for other bacchants.

CHORUS   Many are the shapes of the divine.
Many things the gods achieve that are unexpected.
What seems likely does not come to pass,
But god finds a way for the improbable.   1215
So did these events unfold.

Synopsis of the play

PROLOGUE (1–48)
Dionysus announces himself and his reason for coming to Thebes disguised as the human leader of the Dionysiac cult.

PARODOS (49–142)
The Chorus enter and sing a hymn in honour of Dionysus. They have come to Greece following their cult leader.

FIRST EPISODE (143–291)
Tiresias and Cadmus announce their intention to go to Mount Cithaeron, to dance in honour of Dionysus. Pentheus enters, and is shocked to find these respected elders joining in with the new cult. Tiresias and Cadmus try to win him over to their side, but he rejects them furiously; he orders Tiresias' special seat to be destroyed, and threatens to capture the foreign leader of the cult and put him to death.

FIRST CHORAL ODE (292–346)
The Chorus sing lyrics which comment on the preceding scene. They denounce Pentheus as blasphemous and arrogant, and wish they were somewhere else, far away from such repression. They state the importance of humility and moderation.

SECOND EPISODE (347–433)
A soldier brings Dionysus before Pentheus. This is the first of three confrontations between king and god in the play. Pentheus interrogates the stranger angrily, but Dionysus remains calm in the face of imprisonment.

SECOND CHORAL ODE (434–78)
The Chorus, their leader imprisoned, sing a song of tribulation. They appeal to Thebes, affirm faith in their worship, denounce Pentheus again, and pray to Dionysus to appear and save them.

THIRD EPISODE (479–727)
As though in answer to the Chorus' prayer, the palace is shaken by a violent earthquake, and Dionysus' voice is heard crying from within. He appears again as the cult leader, and Pentheus comes looking for his escaped prisoner. He is shocked by the events, and at a loss trying to control the fearless stranger. When Dionysus offers to take him to spy

on the bacchants, Pentheus is almost literally entranced by the idea, and increasingly falls under the god's power.

THIRD CHORAL ODE (728–70)
The Chorus express their reaction to the events, and hope for revenge against Pentheus. They insist that the gods cannot be mocked with impunity.

FOURTH EPISODE (771–37)
Dionysus leads Pentheus back out of the palace. The king, now dressed as a woman as well as a worshipper of Dionysus, has been reduced to a pathetic state of delusion. He is entirely in Dionysus' power, and the god mocks him by humouring his fancies.

FOURTH CHORAL ODE (838–80)
The Chorus sing a song of vengeance. They sing to inspire the bacchants with rage against Pentheus, and then describe the events on the mountain as though they could see them.

FIFTH EPISODE (881–978)
A messenger arrives from Cithaeron. He describes the journey of Pentheus and Dionysus to the mountain, Pentheus' capture by the women, and his death.

FIFTH CHORAL ODE (979–96)
The Chorus sing a song of triumph at the announcement of Pentheus' death.

EXODOS (997–1216)
The mad Agave arrives carrying the head of her son Pentheus, and the Chorus speak to her. Although they had previously seen her as their enemy, they pity her now. Cadmus arrives from the mountain with the pieces of Pentheus' body. He talks to Agave and helps her recover her senses. They express their grief at what has happened. Dionysus appears above the stage as himself, the god. The two mortals express their grief, but Dionysus justifies and distances himself. Cadmus and Agave address their final laments to each other, and leave to follow their daunting destinies.

Pronunciation of names

To attempt an authentic pronunciation of Classical Greek names presents great difficulties. It is perhaps easiest to accept the conventional anglicised versions of the familiar names (e.g. Zeus). The key below offers help with all the names in the play, which will give a reasonable overall consistency. Note that the stress occurs on the italicised syllable.

> **KEY**
> *ay* – as in 'hay'
> *ai* – as in 'hair'
> *ō* – long 'o', as in 'go'
>
> *ch* – as in Scottish 'loch'
> *ie* – as in 'die'

Achelous	A-chel-*ō*-us	Euios	*E*-wi-os
Acheron	A-cher-*ōn*	Hera	*Hai*-ra
Actaeon	Ak-*tie*-ōn	Hysiae	*Hi*-si-ie
Agave	A-*gah*-wai	Iacchus	I-*a*-kus
Agenor	A-*gai*-nōr	Ino	*Ee*-nō
Aphrodite	A-fro-*die*-tai	Ismenus	Is-*mee*-nus
Apollo	A-*poll*-ō	Loxias	*Lok*-si-as
Ares	*Air*-eez	Lydia	*Li*-di-a
Aristaeus	A-rist-*tie*-us	Lydias	*Li*-di-as
Artemis	*Ar*-te-mis	Lyssa	*Lis*-sa
Asopus	A-*sō*-pus	Maenad	*Mie*-nad
Autonoë	Aw-*ton*-o-ai	Medes	Meeds
Axios	*Ak*-si-os	Olympus	O-*lim*-pus
Bacchus	*Bak*-kus	Orpheus	*Or*-fe-us
Bromios	*Brom*-i-os	Pentheus	*Pen*-the-us
Cadmus	*Kad*-mus	Phoebus	*Fee*-bus
Cithaeron	Ki-*thie*-rōn	Phrygia	*Fri*-ji-a
Corybants	*Ko*-ri-bants	Pieria	Pi-*e*-ri-a
Corycia	Ko-*ri*-si-a	Sardis	*Sar*-dis
Cronus	*Kro*-nus	Satyr	*Sa*-ter
Curetes	Koo-*ree*-tees	Semele	*Se*-me-lee
Cybele	*Si*-be-lee	Sidon	*Sie*-dōn
Delphi	*Del*-fi	Thebes	Theebs
Demeter	De-*mee*-ter	Thessaly	*Thes*-sa-li
Dionysus	Die-o-*nie*-sus	Tiresias	Tie-*re*-si-as
Dirce	*Der*-see	Tmolus	*Tmō*-lus
Echion	E-chi-ōn	Zeus	Zyoos
Erythrae	E-*ri*-thrie		

Introduction to the Greek Theatre

Theātron, the Greek word that gave us 'theatre' in English, meant both 'viewing place' and the assembled viewers. These ancient viewers (*theātai*) were in some ways very different from their modern counterparts. For a start, they were participants in a religious festival, and they went to watch plays only on certain days in the year, when shows were put on in honour of Dionysus. At Athens, where drama developed many of its most significant traditions, the main Dionysus festival, held in the spring, was one of the most important events in the city's calendar, attracting large numbers of citizens and visitors from elsewhere in the Greek world. It is not known for certain whether women attended; if any did, they were more likely to be visitors than the wives of Athenian citizens.

The festival was also a great sporting occasion. Performances designed to win the god's favour needed spectators to witness and share in the event, just as the athletic contests did at Olympia or Delphi, and one of the ways in which the spectators got involved was through competition. What they saw were three sets of three tragedies plus a satyr play, five separate comedies and as many as twenty song-and-dance performances called dithyrambs, put on in honour of Dionysus by choruses representing the different 'tribes' into which the citizen body was divided. There was a contest for each different event, with the dithyramb choruses divided into men's and boys' competitions, and a panel of judges determined the winners. The judges were appointed to act on behalf of the city; no doubt they took some notice of the way the audience responded on each occasion. Attendance at these events was on a large scale: we should be thinking of football crowds rather than typical theatre audiences in the modern world.

Like football matches, dramatic festivals were open-air occasions, and the performances were put on in daylight rather than with stage lighting in a darkened auditorium. The ideal performance space in these circumstances was a hollow hillside to seat spectators, with a flat area at the bottom (*orchēstra*) in which the chorusmen could spread out for their dancing and singing and which could be closed off by a stage-building (*skēnē*) acting simultaneously as backdrop, changing-room and sounding-board. Effective acoustics and good sight-lines were achieved by the kind of design represented in Fig. A on page 98, which shows the Theatre of Dionysus at Athens. The famous stone theatre at Epidaurus (Fig. B on page 98), built about 330 BC, and often taken as typical, has a circular *orchēstra,* but in the fifth century it was normal practice for theatres to have a low wooden stage in front of the *skēnē,* for use by the actors, who also interacted with the chorus in the *orchēstra.*

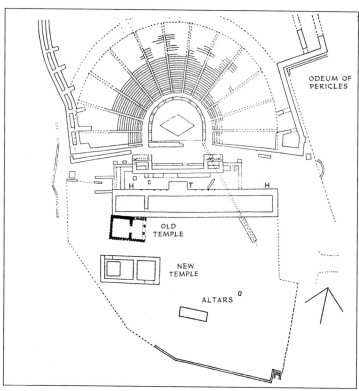

Fig. A. *The Theatre and Sanctuary of Dionysus at Athens.*

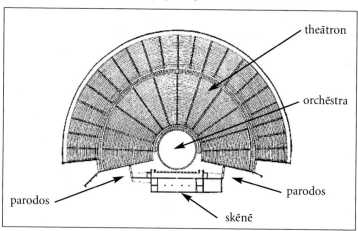

Fig. B. *The Theatre at Epidaurus (4th century BC).*

Song and dance by choruses and the accompanying music of the piper were integral to all these types of performance and not just to the dithyramb. In tragedy there were 12 (later 15) chorusmen, in comedy 24, and in dithyramb 50; plays were often named after their chorus: Aeschylus' *Persians*, Euripides' *Bacchae*, Aristophanes' *Birds* are familiar examples. The rhythmic movements, groupings and singing of the chorus contributed crucially to the overall impact of each show, ensuring that there was always an animated stage picture even when only one or two actors were in view. The practice of keeping the number of speaking actors normally restricted to three, with doubling of roles by the same actor where necessary, looks odd at first sight, but it makes sense in the special circumstance of Greek theatrical performance. Two factors are particularly relevant: first the use of masks, which was probably felt to be fundamental to shows associated with the cult of Dionysus and which made it easy for an actor to take more than one part within a single play, and second the need to concentrate the audience's attention by keeping the number of possible speakers limited. In a large open acting area some kind of focusing device is important if the spectators are always to be sure where to direct their gaze. The Greek plays that have survived, particularly the tragedies, are extremely economical in their design, with no sub-plots or complications in the action which audiences might find distracting or confusing. Acting style, too, seems to have relied on large gestures and avoidance of fussy detail; we know from the size of some of the surviving theatres that many spectators would be sitting too far away to catch small-scale gestures or stage business. Some plays make powerful use of props, like Ajax's sword, Philoctetes' bow, or the head of Pentheus in *Bacchae*, but all these are carefully chosen to be easily seen and interpreted.

Above all, actors seem to have depended on their highly trained voices in order to captivate audiences and stir their emotions. By the middle of the fifth century there was a prize for the best actor in the tragic competition, as well as for the playwright and the financial sponsor of the performance (*chorēgos*), and comedy followed suit a little later. What was most admired in the leading actors who were entitled to compete for this prize was the ability to play a series of different and very demanding parts in a single day and to be a brilliant singer as well as a compelling speaker of verse: many of the main parts involve solo songs or complex exchanges between actor and chorus. Overall, the best plays and performances must have offered audiences a great charge of energy and excitement: the chance to see a group of chorusmen dancing and singing in a sequence of different guises, as young maidens, old counsellors, ecstatic maenads, and exuberant satyrs; to watch scenes in which supernatural beings – gods, Furies, ghosts – come into contact with human beings; to listen to intense debates and hear the blood-curdling offstage cries that heralded the arrival of a messenger with an account of terrifying deeds within, and then to see the bodies brought out and witness the lamentations. Far more 'happened' in most plays than we can easily imagine from the bare text on the page; this must help to account for the continuing appeal of drama throughout antiquity and across the Greco-Roman world.

From the fourth century onwards dramatic festivals became popular wherever there were communities of Greek speakers, and other gods besides Dionysus were honoured with performances of plays. Actors, dancers and musicians organised themselves for professional touring – some of them achieved star status and earned huge fees – and famous old plays were revived as part of the repertoire. Some of the plays that had been first performed for Athenian citizens in the fifth century became classics for very different audiences – women as well as men, Latin speakers as well as Greeks – and took on new kinds of meaning in their new environment. But theatre was very far from being an antiquarian institution: new plays, new dramatic forms like mime and pantomime, changes in theatre design, staging, masks and costumes all demonstrate its continuing vitality in the Hellenistic and Roman periods. Nearly all the Greek plays that have survived into modern times are ones that had a long theatrical life in antiquity; this perhaps helps to explain why modern actors, directors and audiences have been able to rediscover their power.

For further reading: entries in *Oxford Classical Dictionary* (3rd edition) under 'theatre staging, Greek' and 'tragedy, Greek'; J.R. Green, 'The theatre', Ch. 7 of *The Cambridge Ancient History, Plates to Volumes V and VI*, Cambridge, 1994; Richard Green and Eric Handley, *Images of the Greek Theatre*, London, 1995; Rush Rehm, *Greek Tragic Theatre*, London and New York, 1992; P.E. Easterling (ed.), *The Cambridge Companion to Greek Tragedy*, Cambridge, 1997; David Wiles, *Tragedy in Athens*, Cambridge, 1997.

P.E. Easterling

Time line

Dates of selected authors and extant works

12th century BC	**The Trojan war**	
8th century BC	**HOMER**	• *The Iliad* • *The Odyssey*
5th century BC 490–479 431–404	**The Persian wars** **The Peloponnesian wars**	

c. 525/4–456/5
 	
472
 	
456
	AESCHYLUS	(In possible order.)
		
		• *Persians*
		• *Seven against Thebes*
		• *Suppliants*
		• **Oresteia Trilogy**:
		  Agamemnon, Choephoroi
		  Eumenides
		• *Prometheus Bound*

c. 496/5–406 409 401 (posthumous)	**SOPHOCLES**	(Undated plays are in alphabetical order.) • *Ajax* • *Oedipus Tyrannus* • *Antigone* • *Trachiniae* • *Electra* • *Philoctetes* • *Oedipus at Colonus*
c. 490/80–407/6 438 (1st production 455) 431 428 415 412 409 ?408 ?408–6	**EURIPIDES**	(In probable order.) • *Alcestis* • *Medea* • *Heracleidae* • *Hippolytus* • *Andromache* • *Hecuba* • *Suppliant Woman* • *Electra* • *Trojan Women* • *Heracles* • *Iphigenia among the Taurians* • *Helen* • *Ion* • *Phoenissae* • *Orestes* • *Cyclops* (satyr-play) • *Bacchae* • *Iphigenia at Aulis*
460/450–*c.* 386 411 405	**ARISTOPHANES**	• *Thesmophoriazusae* • *Lysistrata* • *Frogs*
4th century BC 384–322	**ARISTOTLE**	• *The Art of Poetry*

Index

Numbers refer to lines, unless **bold** (page).